STOP THE WORLD!

I WANT TO TELL SOMEONE OFF!

Janet Cantor Gari

Stop The World — I Want To Tell Someone Off!
© 2011 Janet Cantor Gari. All Rights Reserved.

No part of this book may be reproduced in any form or by any means, electronic, mechanical, digital, photocopying or recording, except for the inclusion in a review, without permission in writing from the publisher.

Published in the USA by:
BearManor Media
PO Box 1129
Duncan, Oklahoma 73534-1129
www.bearmanormedia.com

ISBN 978-1-59393-671-6

Printed in the United States of America.
Book design by Brian Pearce | Red Jacket Press.

TABLE OF CONTENTS

Preface 7
I Love A Piano 9
A Wild Goose Chase To Turkey 13
Red Riding Hood Revisited 19
The Birth of The Blues 23
Scout's Honor 27
Dire Education 31
Vanity Will Get You Everywhere 35
Groupies 39
Is It Something We Said? 43
And Justice For All 47
Bedtime Story 49
Catalogs 53
The Pen Isn't Always Mightier 57
Hollywood Hack 61
Scam Boomerang 65
Shipping and Manhandling 69
Not A Clue 73
The Eyes Have It 77
A Midsummer Night's Scheme 81
A House Is Not A Home 85
South of The Border 89

Getting A Ticket	91
At Your Service	93
Innocent Bystander	95
A Bit O' Blarney	97
Just Say No	99
Fiddler On A Hot Tin Roof	103
Brown Bagging It	107
At Odds With Nature	111
Those Who Can't...	115
Calling A Spade A Spade	119
Petty Politics	121
Sex and The Silly	125
To Soothe The Savage Breast	129
Socializing	133
Underground Adventures	137
Independence Day	141
Insurance	145
Take a Letter	149
There's No Business Like...	153
Ladies Who Lunch	157
Scrabble	161
Jumping The Gun	165
Where's My Parachute?	169
The Way To Whose Heart?	171
Efficiency	175
Where Celldom Is Heard	177
The Twilight Zone	181
The Hills Are Alive	185

PREFACE

It would seem from the following collection of anecdotes that I'm perennially "scamatose," but all of these episodes occurred over a period of many years. I found that it may be easy to grow up, but it's not easy to wise up.

All of these deceits are true. I've written them down, because many of my friends found them to be so ludicrous that, even though they were sympathetic, they laughed out loud.

I have also included situations that I find to be outrageous, even if they're not scams or practical jokes. Thus, the title: *Stop the World — I Want to Tell Someone Off!*

This is by no means a book "you just can't put down." It's not a story with a beginning, middle and an end. It's just an accumulation of accurate, but miscellaneous, memories I'd like to share with you.

Feel free to contest any of my opinions. As Ben Ohmart will attest, this is not written in stone — they're paperback!

I Love A Piano

When my daughter went off to college in Boston, and my son was already making a living at songwriting and performing, I decided it was time for me to move to midtown from the Upper West Side. I found a small one-bedroom apartment right in the theatre district and looked forward to my new digs.

There was plenty of furniture in the old apartment to fill my new home without leaving my son in bare rooms, but I didn't think I would be able to fit our baby grand piano and decided to sell it, buying, instead, a spinet like the one my son owned.

I put an ad in the *Times* and got a few nibbles and one solid offer. It was from an actress who was not a star, but who worked all the time in small parts and a few commercials. She came over, looked at the piano, ran her fingers "o'er the keys" and promptly made out a check for the full amount. She then asked if her movers could arrive for pickup the very next day. I was going away for the weekend, but told her my son would let them in.

This was on a Friday, but I was able to get to the bank in time to deposit her check. I know what you're thinking, and you're right! Monday I got a call from my bank that her check had bounced. I immediately called her bank for an explanation and was told that she had been in arrears for six months! I called her at once, and she sounded shocked (well, she *was* an actress) and said she would have a certified check ready for me that very afternoon if I could pick it up on the street in front of her apartment on 72nd Street. When I rang her downstairs bell, there was no answer, so I rang someone else's bell and got inside. I climbed the stairs feeling very uneasy and pictured finding her body! Yes, I watch a lot of cop shows. Instead, I found a stack of unopened mail in front of her door, but no sign of the woman herself.

She had disappeared, but so had my piano!

About a week later I got a call from an actor friend who knew my story, informing me that there on the Equity bulletin board was an ad listing a baby grand piano for sale — with her name boldly attached, as well as a phone number. He agreed to pretend to be a potential buyer and phoned her at once. She said the piano was in a Brooklyn warehouse, but that if he would pick her up where she was temporarily living, she would take him there to examine it. When he asked the name of the apartment's owner (she said she was babysitting two little girls), I guess she got suspicious, and she canceled their meeting.

My same friend, who was also a good actor, agreed to call her in a different voice and say that he was from Con Edison. A gas leak had been reported. She seemed genuinely concerned and requested an inspection as soon as possible.

Meanwhile, I had gone to a Criminal Court judge and gotten a subpoena for her to appear on a certain date. I had also told my story to a local policeman, who agreed to serve her, but who said I had to stay out of sight until she came to the door, so that I could positively identify her.

There I stood in the shadow of the mail chute, my heart thumping so hard I thought it would burst. I had seen private eyes only in the movies, and they were always muscle men, not timid little women who didn't know what to expect. Sure enough, the thief herself opened the door with the two little girls clinging to her, and I left my hiding place, actually apologizing to her for this necessary intrusion. She agreed to appear.

On the way out, the cop remarked, "That's some tough cookie. Bet she never shows up."

He was wrong. When I got to the courthouse, she was already there, and our case was next on the docket. She came over to me with the full amount of cash in her hand and asked if I would drop the charges. I pocketed the money, canceled the case, and we rode home together on the subway, amiably chatting about clothes and makeup!

Two weeks later my actor friend called to say that there was another notice on the Equity bulletin board. The phone number was the same, but this time the items for sale were a couch, a coffee table and a typewriter.

A Wild Goose Chase To Turkey

It's not easy to raise money to produce a show — even a very small budget show, but I had taken on the project, and I was determined.

An actor friend of mine had been working in Florida and had struck up an acquaintance with the young woman renting the condo next to his. He described the show to her, and she said that by coincidence she would be phoning a friend of hers that night who had excellent connections. They agreed to get together after his performance, and he would meet the money source long distance.

The long distance friend, in turn, suggested that he have me call the owner of a meat-packing plant in New Jersey, who, if he liked the project, would finally introduce me to the "angel."

It all sounded extremely complicated to me, but I was game. I sent a tape of the musical to my New Jersey contact, and we had several conversations about what the show's budget entailed, as he had listened to the tape with enormous enthusiasm and had been in touch with HIM, as he will be referred to from now on, since that was the only identification I was ever to know.

I had already signed with a theatrical lawyer and a general manager and was looking for no other input besides backing, with the usual incentive of a larger percentage of the show to the backer if he were indeed the sole source.

One day, out of the blue, I got a call from the New Jersey meat-packer. He had spoken to HIM, and I was to leave for Turkey the following morning! "You won't come back with a check in your pocket," he warned, "but you will come back fully funded. By the way, you don't have to kiss HIS ring or anything, because, after all, you're an American, but you should bring a gift."

"Myrrh?" I asked. "Frankincense? Gold?"

Very seriously he responded that "HE would love to have a Natalie Cole album, and HIS assistant needs some new mascara."

Within two hours the round-trip plane ticket arrived by messenger from a travel agency. My lawyer was skeptical, but didn't seem too worried about my going, but my friends were terribly concerned. One of them insisted that I at least give him the phone number where I could be reached, and I gave him the only number I had — that which the contact of the contact of the contact had given me. She was now in Turkey herself and told me that I would be picked up at the airport by HIS limo and would be staying at the Istanbul Hilton.

I couldn't believe that I, who would rather not travel as far as the Bronx, was going to Turkey. I packed carefully, could hardly sleep that night and stayed awake for the entire plane trip, memorizing every word of the limited partnership papers to be able to answer any question that might come up.

I filled myself full of coffee during the stopover in Rome and was extremely jittery, but definitely wide awake when we arrived in Istanbul. Looking around the airport in vain for a limo, I noticed a bedraggled American-looking young woman, and as I got closer, I saw she was holding up a cardboard sign with my name on it. She introduced herself as Mary, the one my actor friend had spoken to long distance from Florida, and said that HIS limo was in use by some government officials, so she had come to get me by taxi, since I would not be staying at the Hilton, but rather at her apartment.

We got into the cab, and the motion of the vehicle over the sometimes bumpy roads counteracted the coffee and made me so sleepy that I found it almost unbearable to keep my eyes open. Abruptly she announced that we were going to see the mosques. When I suggested that we get an early start the next day, if we were going to sightsee, she said it had to be at that moment, because we couldn't go to her apartment in the American sector until the guard came on duty. I was suddenly ready to commute to the Bronx daily.

When the cab dropped us off, we were still a few minutes early for the guard, so we went next door to a 7-Eleven, of all things, and drank Turkish coffee. Finally, it was time to go upstairs. The edifice looked more like an office building than an apartment house, but I really didn't care at this point, hoping for an hour's nap before I got any more surprises. We climbed a beautiful marble staircase with a polished oak banister to the second floor, where Mary unlocked one door only to reveal a second one just like it. "The first one's for bombs," she said matter-of-factly.

We entered a strange living room which contained normal-looking furniture for the most part, but heavy, heavy fitness equipment on one side. Mary put on the tape of the show and pointed out the bathroom, "my" room, her room and the kitchen. She said I'd have plenty of time for a nap before HE arrived.

I fell asleep immediately and awoke exactly one hour later to find the tape still playing (auto reverse, I assume), but no sign of Mary. Her large bed was made, but her clothes all seemed to be in suitcases, with only a coat or two hanging in her closet. The clock on the electric stove was blinking 12:00, as if it had never been set. The refrigerator contained only a bottle of water. I really began to panic when I saw her purse still on the couch where she had dropped it, and I searched through it frantically to see if she had taken her keys or if someone had taken her. The keys were gone, and the only phone in the apartment was obviously a house phone.

Carefully I opened both sets of doors and made sure they wouldn't close behind me. Then I crept down the stairs to do I don't know what. Fortunately, a woman was coming in with two little children. I asked her if she knew Mary, and she understood enough English to laugh and point across the street. There was Mary, talking on the phone in a taxi stand and waving merrily to me, gesturing that she would be right there. That phone number, by the way, was the one I had so trustingly given my friend at home — a phone in a taxi stand!

Mary returned, asked if I had a good nap and said HE wouldn't be coming over until later, so we should go out to dinner. I guess she didn't think a bottle of water would be sufficient. We went next door to a Turkish pizza place, where, I must say, I had the most delicious pizza I've ever had — far from anything Italian, but very spicy and well cooked.

When we returned to the apartment, Mary changed into an even more rumpled blouse and pants, and we sat down to wait for HIM. We talked mostly about politics, and every time I'd try to get around to the show, she'd delve into my opinion of the general American attitude toward every country I've ever heard of and some I didn't know existed.

Finally, I heard the key in the door, and HE arrived — no long robes, bejeweled fingers or satin slippers. He was a young version of Omar Sharif, dressed in chinos and a sport shirt and flashing the whitest teeth I'd ever seen. HE would flash them a lot during the hours to follow.

HE, too, wanted to talk only about politics, and when I brought up the show, HE waved it aside as if it were the last thing on HIS mind (which I'm sure it was). HE then graciously offered to take us to dinner, so Mary changed into a dress so wrinkled I thought maybe that was how the fabric had been designed.

We went to a nearby open-air restaurant with a beautiful view, and HE ordered a delicious semi-sweet wine, but what was the dinner? Pizza!

When we returned to the apartment, the three of us talked the night through, and I finally begged off at 5:00AM. He mumbled something about getting a cab, but when I awoke at 2:00 in the afternoon, there he was in the kitchen. Mary, in yet another unpressed outfit, was making him breakfast. She invited me to join them, and I was delighted to find some toast to eat, because whatever they were having looked as if it might still be alive.

At last HE agreed to talk business. HE put on the tape, playing it so loudly that we had to shout over it to hear each other. HE would not consider either my lawyer or my general manager, HE stated flatly. HE would be in charge of everything or there would be no deal. I told HIM quite calmly that HE could not have creative control, and HE sneered that HE had no interest in that — just the business side.

HE went on to tell me that HE had lived in New York for five years and was immensely successful as a producer, although HE was adamant about not having HIS name appear on any of the shows that HE named (all the biggest hits of those five years). HE then mentioned that HE had lived not far from my apartment, describing each street in such detail that I began to feel as if I were in an old World War II movie, where the Nazi, posing as an American soldier, memorizes perfectly all the baseball scores and players' name and nicknames in order to slip by.

Then the two of them went at me full force with their political brainwashing, warning me that the CIA was about to take over the United States and that I should get out while the getting was still possible. I still didn't know what they wanted from me and will probably never know, but I was extremely relieved when the downstairs bell rang. It was the taxi to take me to the airport.

"What about the show?" I asked in a last futile attempt.

"There she goes again," HE answered, flashing his white teeth as a farewell.

I hoped with all my heart that the taxi driver was indeed taking me to the airport, and I was so grateful when that is where we arrived that I tipped him with all the Turkish money I had left. He was very happy.

As I approached the check-in counter, a beautiful young woman in a uniform asked for my passport in English too perfect to be real, and I realized that she had worked as hard on her accent as she had on her grooming. First, she noted the short time I had spent in her country. I told her I was there on business.

"What is your business?" she asked.

"Show business," I answered. "You know, 'There's no business like show business.'" (A little joke I knew she wouldn't get.)

She raised her eyebrows in question.

I mimed an audience applauding, and she understood.

"Where did you stay?" she asked.

"I don't know," I answered honestly. "I couldn't read the name of the street, and I was picked up at the airport by the person with whom I stayed."

"And who was that?"

"Mary O'Reilly."

"What does she do?"

There she had me, because I didn't know if Mary was a spy, a terrorist, a political analyst or just a sloppy dresser. I didn't dare hesitate, though, because the last thing I wanted was to be detained for any kind of questioning.

Boldly I stated, "She's a fallderand."

"Excuse me?"

"A fallderand."

I had gambled, and it had worked. I made up a word and knew that the lovely young investigator didn't want to admit that her understanding of English was so limited. The poor thing probably spent that entire night poring over dictionaries and encyclopedias trying to find at least a synonym.

Without another word she stamped my passport, and I was on my way home — no check in my pocket and no funding, but on my way home.

Maybe this would make a good musical. I wonder where I could get backing…

Red Riding Hood Revisited

Once upon a time Little Red Riding Hood wrote to her delighted grandmother to say that she was coming for a visit. Her grandmother didn't live in the woods, but in a small New York City apartment with an even smaller kitchen.

"Since we'll both be using the kitchen, what can I do to make my granddaughter's visit more comfortable?" thought her grandmother. "I know," she decided. "I can't make the room bigger, but I can make it more compact."

Now, Red's grandma had always lived in rented apartments, so she had no experience with renovations of any kind. Early on she had bought a convertible sofa and a fold-out table and even had a canvas wardrobe that could be assembled in minutes. These items had all been bought at department stores, however, and therefore required no expert advice or installation.

Grandma scanned the classifieds, as she would for any other service, such as take-out food or flower delivery. My, but there were a lot of "kitchen renovators!" Each one declared they were licensed and insured. Grandmother called the four nearest her home for a "free estimate." She asked the first one who arrived if it were possible to put a microwave/convection oven on the wall, with a dishwasher underneath, and four freestanding burners, either gas or electric.

The "contractor" spoke knowledgeably about the rewiring that he would do, the shelf that he would build and the appliances that he would purchase at "his" discount. He scribbled down many figures and asked for a down payment for half of the full amount of his service, explaining that he needed it to buy the appliances.

Grandmother, a sophisticated New Yorker in other aspects of her life, was incredibly naïve in this area and promptly gave him a check for the amount he requested. He gave her his cell phone number and faxed her a contract on which he acknowledged her down payment.

That was the last Red's grandmother ever saw of Mr. Wolf. He would call almost every week to set up an appointment for delivery and cancel it the day before he was due to arrive. Just as Grandma was about to accuse him of fraud, she was delayed by a near-fatal heart attack and a triple bypass. Mr. Wolf was most sympathetic when she called him upon her return home from the hospital, and he attempted once again to continue his scam. One day he carelessly called from his home, leaving a traceable number on Grandma's Caller ID, which led to an address and an alternate company name. Grandma, frail as she was, managed to sue him in Small Claims Court.

As one might expect, Mr. Wolf stayed in his lair on the day of the hearing, and Grandmother received a default judgment in her favor.

Satisfying the judgment, however, was another story entirely. The Sheriff had the responsibility of collecting the money, but not of finding it. Instead of playing "Break the Bank," Grandmother found herself playing "Find the Bank." On the very day Mr. Wolf received the summons from Small Claims Court, he closed the account in which he had deposited Grandma's check, and he closed every subsequent account the minute Grandma found it.

At the suggestion of Grandma's son — not a woodsman, but a musician — Grandma called ABC's 7 on Your Side. Although they did not recover the misappropriated money, they did make several calls to Mr. Wolf. Annoyed with them, and perhaps fearing that their huffing and puffing might actually blow his house down, he delivered a postdated check to Grandma. The check would have been of no use whatsoever, but he inadvertently gave away the secret of his bank's whereabouts.

Upon advice from the Sheriff, Grandma borrowed one of the waterproof red hooded capes that her granddaughter had left and set out in the rain to Small Claims Court once again, obtaining a restraining order, valid for a year, to freeze Mr. Wolf's account, giving the Sheriff plenty of time to get an execution judgment from the judge for collection.

After several threats from Mr. Wolf, both on the phone and in the mail, an indignant Grandmother called the local police precinct, and a detective pointed out to Mr. Wolf that he would be arrested if he ever contacted Grandma again.

What a happy day it was when the check arrived — the original amount plus interest and expenses. The nightmare of a year and a half had ended. Grandma then asked the right questions of the right people and renovated the kitchen herself — for half the amount Mr. Wolf would have charged.

Moral: Wolves who prey on grandmas may find that sweet little old ladies aren't as sweet as they used to be.

Warning To Other Grandmas: Ads in the phone book are not screened for truth or accuracy.

The Birth of The Blues

Thank heaven things have changed since I had my kids. My granddaughter sailed through two births and was home and active only two days after each one. They're fifteen months apart -even family planning has been speeded up these days!

One very cold morning in February several years ago, my water broke and my husband called the doctor, helped me to get dressed, bundled me up in my winter coat with a blanket around me like a cape and stashed me in a doorway out of the wind while he hailed a cab.

Unfortunately, it was rush hour, and everyone was going to work. There simply were no cabs to be had, and my contractions were getting closer and closer. Finally, my husband spotted a policeman and explained our situation. The cop promptly stopped a cab, and the passengers *refused* to get out! He threatened them with arrest (I don't know on what grounds), and we were on our way to the hospital.

While my husband filled out the insurance and admittance forms, I assumed everything was going to be more comfortable and reassuring from then on. No way! We were sent up to the maternity floor, and I was ushered into a cubicle and told to put on a hospital gown and put my clothes in a paper bag. The nurse then handed the bag to my husband and ordered me to say goodbye from the cubicle — no kisses or hugs or good luck wishes. He reluctantly walked away, and I was sure I was going to be exterminated.

Upon giving me the preliminary examination, the nurse demanded an answer: "When did you break your membrane?" Not being familiar with any medical terms whatsoever, I replied innocently, "We were in a terrible rush, but I don't think I broke anything."

Things proceeded on that ultra-friendly basis until my son was finally born. I was surprised they even allowed his father to meet him, but we both held him happily, and my husband said he'd be back at visiting hour that night.

I promptly fell asleep and awoke refreshed and alert. After all, I hadn't had ether or anything, so I had just been exhausted, not drugged.

When my husband returned that evening, he found that his cousin, two doors down the hall, had also given birth, and she had a roomful of visitors who were delighted to see him. The whole gang decided to visit me, too, and we were having a merry old time when a vendor came by with a cart selling deli sandwiches and drinks. No one had told me that the little bowl of Jell-O they had given me was supposed to be my dinner, and I was very, very hungry, so when they ordered, I did, too — a huge deli sandwich and a milk shake.

Also, no one told me I'd get sick from a full meal; I didn't, not for a minute!

It was a very hot september day when I went back to the same hospital to give birth to my daughter. The same resident was in charge of the labor room, and he chuckled indulgently when I said my arms and legs were hurting a lot. "You're in labor," he reminded me. "That must be referred pain."

I had the baby and slept soundly until the next day, when I had a couple of visitors, including my music teacher. I had not yet even seen my baby. I was chatting with him until I got so cold I asked him to get another blanket from the nurse. By the time he got back, I was burning hot, and they called the doctor, who came at once. He looked very worried, took my temperature and a couple of tests and left.

I called for the nurse, who would not answer any questions, but said to wait for the doctor. Frantically, I managed to get my father on the phone. He and my mother had come into town for the birth and were staying at a hotel. I knew my husband would be there with them.

"Don't worry, honey," my father said. "You have a bad case of the flu and a very high temperature. That's why they won't bring the baby to you. We've seen her; she's very cute."

No one at the hospital could have told me that?

Scout's Honor

When my daughter was very young, she suddenly got an urge to join the Girl Scouts. Inasmuch as she was, like the rest of my family, totally disinterested in sports and all physical activities except swimming, I think it must have been the cookies that intrigued her.

However, she was trustworthy, loyal, friendly, kind, cheerful, reverent, courteous, obedient, thrifty, brave, helpful and clean. I don't know about the "obedient," but she fit the rest of the organization oath.

She did have me write her an excuse to avoid an overnight stay at a camp site, but she tried to keep up with other requests.

In addition to the regular promotion of Girl Scout cookies, the girls were requested to make things to be offered at the bake sale. Excitedly, my eager child asked if she and I could make cupcakes. Easy enough! I chose a rich chocolate recipe which would not require icing. We measured, mixed and poured, putting our product into the oven.

The cupcakes rose beautifully, and when they came out of the oven, we let them cool long enough to be able remove them from the pan and cool completely on a platter.

Since it was getting quite late, I suggested that we let them cool overnight and pack them up in the morning. We covered them with a light cotton dishcloth and went to bed.

Unbeknownst to us, another creature was not sleeping as yet. Our cat had slipped into the kitchen sniffing the baking aroma and had leaped up on the counter as soon as we left. Fortunately, she made no attempt to lift the towel, but she thought the warmth was there for her benefit, so she settled herself on top and went to sleep for the night.

She had jumped down by morning, but what we found was a platter full of cupcakes that were flattened like an old-fashioned top hat. At first we were mystified, but when we looked more closely, we could see the outline of the cat's body on the towel!

The sweets were due that morning, but we couldn't deliver that ridiculous collection. Quickly, I whipped up a large bowl of thick icing, tinted a much darker pink than I had thought I was mixing, and spooned it on the squashed cupcakes. My daughter got into the spirit and added bright green sprinkles. They were probably the ugliest confections I'd ever seen and not what we had promised at all. Of course, we couldn't wrap them while they were still moist, so we put them in an open box side by side, and pretended that the final result was what we meant all along.

We edged our way into a cab, balancing the box, and my daughter later told me they were the first entries to be sold — all of them!

Dire Education

My father never went beyond the sixth grade, but he had had enough of the fundamentals to get along in the world with basic arithmetic. He was very quick to calculate in his head, and my mother, too, was a whiz at figures.

All my sisters and I had been taught in grammar school to add, subtract, multiply and divide. Algebra and geometry were not introduced until high school.

When it was time for my own kids to learn "readin', writin' and 'rithmetic," some raving maniac on some school board got the idea that having humans think like computers instead of the other way around would improve their cerebral capacity.

Thus, the "new math" came into being.

At first I thought it was a one-time assignment, since every problem had to be solved through a zillion estimates and took up at least half a page. What would ordinarily take me no more than a couple of minutes went on and on and on. My children were baffled, so off I went to meet with the principal. I remarked that the kids' little heads were about to explode and that it seemed not only logical, but imperative that basic arithmetic be returned to the basics. My kids were in the majority of those who didn't care "why," but needed to learn "how."

The patronizing answer I received was "*We are the educators,* Mrs. Gari." Undaunted, I replied, "Well, you're not educating." I then announced that I would teach my children at home and that they would solve every single problem on each homework page by themselves, but the papers would be turned in without a detailed description of how they arrived at their answers.

"That is not acceptable," continued the principal. "Oh, well, if it's necessary to sue the school board, I guess that's what I'll have to do," I threatened. Of course, I had no idea if that was possible or even necessary, but it did penetrate his smugness.

On my way out I overheard two teachers talking. One said, "This 'new math' is driving me crazy. I have never had so many requests for conferences in all my years of teaching." The other one agreed, "The kids don't get it; the parents don't get it, and I'm not sure I get it myself!"

Eventually, the entire experiment was dropped, and fortunately my children grew up with a working knowledge of math that gets them through their adult lives with ease.

Another problem was language. The school either refused or was not allowed to hire bilingual teachers, and the majority of students in our local public school were Spanish speaking. This meant that over half of the kids had no idea of what was going on, and it led to a major discipline problem. The PTA was called upon for any available parents to assist in the classroom.

I had studied French, but had no knowledge of Spanish whatsoever, so I volunteered to help out in assemblies. There were tables and chairs and an old piano in the badly neglected assembly room, and the teacher, et al, didn't "enter laughing," but screaming at the top of their voices. I gestured to the teacher to help me move the piano up front and to the children to push back the tables and line up their chairs. Curiosity temporarily overcame their rebelliousness, and when they were settled, I asked in English for them to sing along with me. My thin voice would be backed up at least by a few other sopranos!

I chose Stephen Foster, George M. Cohan and early Irving Berlin — what I felt would be the easiest songs for everyone to follow (and certainly the easiest for me to play!).

After a few awkward moments, those who spoke English joined in, and just a short time later, the rest of the children were chiming in phonetically. I took a quick look at the erstwhile frantic teacher and saw a smile on her now-relaxed face. We were *all* having a good time. Little did I know that this would evolve into an inter-classroom exchange of words amongst the kids themselves and with the teacher.

Today, teaching methods have improved greatly, and my fervent hope is that all our dedicated teachers will be treated fairly and will no longer be pawns in political lunacy.

Vanity Will Get You Everywhere

Having been born with dark circles under my eyes, I put up with them the best I could until I was old enough to cover them with make-up. For the first time in my life I looked as if I had not been on a night-long binge! Three of my sisters were also afflicted. Only Natalie, for some genetic reason, had nothing to distract from her beautiful big green eyes.

Many years ago my sister Marilyn, the black sheep of the family, who was always having something or other done to her face, (no, she never went as far as Michael Jackson, and she didn't dangle her son over a balcony), found a cosmetic surgeon who could, according to her, remove the discoloration once and for all. I didn't realize that she herself was still using a color stick and let her talk me into going to this quack myself.

Although I was not yet old enough for wrinkles (which should have made me wonder just what skin he was going to lift), I listened to his explanation that he would clip the dark circles and lift the remaining under-eye skin up to my lower lashes. This looks good on paper.

I came home with the bruises I had expected, but I was concerned that one eye would not open all the way. In fact, I was beginning to look like that scary character in *The Hitchhiker*. When I pointed this out to the doctor, he advised eye "exercises" of opening my eyes wide and then closing them tightly for 30 seconds several times a day.

By the time I had healed completely, it was obvious that on the one eye he had not only pulled up the skin, but had pulled down the lid to hold it in place. To make matters worse, I found out that dark circles come from the pigment which goes all the way through to the bone and have nothing to do with a layer of skin.

"Why don't you go back and have him do it over?" my friends asked.

"What, and give him another crack at disfiguring me? That's like being hit by a car and standing on the same corner hoping the driver will come around again and miss you this time!"

I went back to using a concealer, but now I have to paint a thicker line on that eye to make it look even with the normal eyeliner on the other one.

And speaking of evening things out, after I was mugged and crippled, I knew I was going to need a lift on my right shoe in order to be able to walk, albeit with a cane or a walker. At the rehab hospital they discussed having orthopedic shoes made, but the samples they showed me were so awfully dreary that I couldn't bear the idea of facing every day with them. I took the measurements home with me and thought of an alternative.

Searching both online and in my catalogs, I found a pair of high-heeled shoes in one location and a pair of matching low-heeled ones or flats in another, so I bought a pair of each in black, brown, navy and taupe (with canvas ones for the summer.) The cost of these double purchases came to about the same amount of money as having the regular orthopedic shoes made.

I deplore the waste. It makes me think of the old joke of the surgeon who is at the bedside of his patient as the patient wakes up. "I have good news and bad news for you," he says.

"What's the bad news?"

"I had to amputate your left foot."

"Well, then, what could possibly be the good news?"

"The fellow in the next bed lost his right foot, and you can share a pair of shoes."

Of course, I can never wear skirts or dresses again, but in pants or jeans it looks as if I'm wearing a normal pair of shoes.

After three operations on my shoulder, for which the surgeon proudly displayed the X-rays to me, I have very little use of my right arm from the elbow to the shoulder. I even reminded the egotistical doctor that it was the old story that "the operation was a success, but the patient died."

Groupies

After my divorce I was very low on self-esteem. Could I have made it work? I had tried for seventeen years. This self-incrimination whirled around in my head for much too long, so I decided to seek help and was directed to a psychologist by a good and trusted friend.

A couple of weeks into my private sessions, the "doctor" insisted that I join his Monday night group. The first night, I quickly explained why I was there and listened to every one else's ongoing situations. The best thing that ever happened to me in that group was that I met two people who were to become lifelong friends. As for any other benefits...

What I found were weekly sessions in which everyone seemed to tell the same stories over and over, and no one seemed to improve or actually to change in any way. Our leader was a short, handsome "happily married" man who kept in great shape, but who chain smoked and encouraged one of the men to bring along his extraordinarily long cigars. I used to wait until everyone was seated and then choose a chair as far away from the cigar as I could find. One night one of the women objected to the unusually strong smell. Quickly, like a defiant child, one of the other men also lit up a stogy. The woman walked out. I regret to this day that I didn't follow her, because the odor was making me nauseous, too. The comment from his highness was that she left because her abusive father had smoked cigars. My father didn't smoke.

The atmosphere gradually became obvious; all the women and all the gay men were madly in love with their master, and the straight men wanted desperately to emulate him. From the very beginning I seemed to be the only one who was immune to his charm. Physically, despite the fact that I'm very small, I have always been attracted to tall, lanky men. Even as a little child, I had a crush on Buddy Ebsen, who was still a young, loose-limbed dancer and should have played the Scarecrow in *The Wizard of Oz*, no matter how terrific Ray Bolger was!

What turned me off the most about the psychologist was his unearned arrogance. Because I came from a show-business family, I thought he was using copious obscenities in our private sessions because he mistakenly assumed that that was the way all show people talked. I didn't realize until much later that he was hitting on me and thought that would turn me on!

He made another error in the group when we were talking about our parents, and I happened to relate a common occurrence in our house. If my father didn't get a laugh from something he said to us, he would turn his back and drop his pants! Naturally, he was fully covered in old-fashioned long boxer shorts. Mother had explained that this was an old burlesque trick — except that the comic in burlesque would be wearing shorts sporting a loud, ridiculous design.

"Aha!" said our all-knowing PhD, "so you were sexually attracted to your father and have been looking for a song-and-dance man ever since." Another goof. My father was a comic who sang; he was never a dancer. Also, my father was only 5'5", and I doubt if even my mother found his boxer shorts sexy!

Most of the characters in the group had been in therapy with the same person for thirty years! Yes, count 'em! I should consider myself lucky that it took me only six years to catch on that instead of helping us to overcome our drawbacks he was playing on our weaknesses to create the impression that we were helpless without his "guidance."

There was one woman who must have heard the old saying "If you want get someone's attention, whisper," and that's what she did. I would spend at least part of every session asking, "What?" She was no longer in love with her husband and said they "lived around each other," but as far as I know, she never did anything about it.

Then there was the young, not particularly attractive, single man, who told the exact same story every Monday about his weekend of unsuccessful dating and going motorcycling with his parents!

One guy tried hard to shock us with his filthy language, but we just called him "gutter mouth," and no one was impressed. He didn't have Tourette's syndrome, but I'm surprised the psychologist didn't diagnose it as that.

Another fellow was into S&M. All of us women were very uncomfortable when he recited his tales, but the men seemed to hang on to every word. That's a compulsion I've never understood. If you like someone enough to want to have sex with him or her, why would you want to administer pain or have it applied to you?

There was one good-looking man who confessed to repeatedly cheating on his wife with all the cute young women in his large office. His excuse was that his wife had let herself go and was dumpy and unattractive. Of course, the group pounced on him for that, but it was only partly an alibi. His wife worked in the same building that I did, and I happened to be in the elevator with her and one of her associates, so I knew who she was, and yes, she was dumpy and unattractive. It was she herself who solved the problem by losing the excess weight and having a makeover. I ran into them at a party, and she was stunning! My dallying group member had fallen in love all over again, and his office "funches," as he called them, were no longer irresistibly appealing. Did the almighty therapist have anything to do with this? No way.

To get closer to my "surprise" ending to this story, I must describe our sex symbol. She was very pretty and had long, gorgeous red hair, which she would toss around very much like displaying the hair care products in today's commercials.

When I announced that I was leaving group, the puppeteer said that I could not continue private sessions unless I stayed. I further astonished him by casually remarking that I intended to leave those sessions, too. He actually called me every day for the next two weeks to "make sure I was all right!" and to welcome me back to private sessions without the group if I cared to return.

Then I read in the paper that he had been having an affair with our sex symbol. He was fined $10,000 and had his license suspended for three months.

But here's the big finish! Everyone else in the group went surreptitiously to his home to cling to their habit until he could go back into practice legally. Could a rock star ask for any more?

Is It Something We Said?

It has been almost twenty years since I lost my dearest friend in the whole world, composer Arthur Siegel. Since I'm a terrible pianist, he used to play any auditions I had when I was still writing only music — and I paid him in brownies! That was before he found that he was diabetic. Brownies and all the other sweets to which he was addicted and still devouring stealthily are what exacerbated his diabetes. It eventually went completely out of control and was the cause of his death.

He was already ill when he was approached to write the music for a show based on true life characters, and he chose me to write the lyrics. We wrote three songs for the producer: a comedy number, a counterpoint duet and a wistful ballad, which we performed for him, and the man was overjoyed with both the words and the music.

Now, about this producer. He was a very, very peculiar person, but Arthur explained that he had indeed gotten a couple of off-Broadway revivals produced, so maybe he was just eccentric. The guy said he was almost finished with his original script and would send us copies as soon as it was complete.

Unfortunately, Arthur was once again hospitalized and didn't want to see anyone except close friends, so he asked the producer to send the script to me and that I would bring it to the hospital.

What arrived was an envelope with only eleven pages, so I assumed that it was just a treatment and that the entire script would follow. I dutifully brought it to the hospital, and Arthur read it and looked at me quizzically.

"Is this an outline, or what?"

"I don't know," I answered. "I'll just have to call him and find out."

When I got him on the phone, I had barely finished my question when he began screaming at me so loudly that I had to hold the phone away, while I tried to make sense out of why he was so angry.

He then phoned Arthur at the hospital, decided I had "influenced" him, called me every name he could think of and said that if he didn't get rid of me, the deal was off!

Not only was the deal off, but Arthur was off the phone as quickly as he could hang it up.

"He's just too crazy for me," Arthur said. "I don't know how anyone has ever worked with him. Maybe because he's only done revivals and has never written anything before, he simply doesn't get it, but as much as I love our songs, I'm glad we're out of it."

I still have the rough tape we made at Arthur's apartment for the Nutty Producer, and occasionally I'll listen to it, but it makes me miss Arthur all the more.

And Justice For All

When I was young, I was employed by Universal Pictures as a secretary in their legal department, so all I knew was about contracts, releases and billing, etc. I didn't know that any private citizen can sue any other private citizen for any amount at any time!

Of course, a judge can throw out the case as frivolous right off the bat, but if she or he doesn't, it can drag on for years, costing the accused a fortune if he or she doesn't qualify for legal aid.

The lowest a complainant can sink is to notify the IRS anonymously that the case is based on fraud by the defendant, and that is exactly what happened to a relative of mine.

Eventually he had to settle (at least it was for a sum far below what was originally the amount sought), because the fees paid to his lawyer and his accountant had left him with not enough capital to continue.

This same sort of scam happened to my sisters and me, when my father's accountant, thirteen years after my father's death, said he had never paid him for doing all our taxes! When we ignored his demand, he called me and said it wouldn't look very nice if it came out in the newspaper that my father was a deadbeat. Daddy was a guy who paid every bill the day it came in the mail. The stock market crash had taught him to be extra careful.

"Hmmmmmn," I answered calmly. "That sounds like extortion to me."

"Don't get out of character!" was his comeback.

"You mean the character I was as an innocent child? I'm an adult now, and we don't owe you anything."

The case was thrown out, but he appealed it, and our lawyer advised us to settle and not throw any more money away. So we did — for a fourth of his claim. The court system had aided him in being a pickpocket

Bedtime Story

Moving from a large apartment to a much smaller one meant scaling down the size of the furniture. A king-size bed took up practically my entire bedroom, so I exchanged with my son and installed the ¾-size bed he had had since he was a teenager!

Apparently, he loved the old mattress that was so saggy it made sleeping on it like lying in a hammock. I admit it was sort of pleasant being hugged on both sides, but I knew it was time to put it to rest in order to give *me* some rest.

There were no memorable commercials on television at the time, so I just wandered in and out of stores that sold bedding until I came to one that carried what I believed, without consulting Goldilocks, was just right. I did the usual — sitting on it, lying on it and checking out the covering.

I was given a delivery date and removed my old mattress (that service was not included in the deal). The new mattress arrived on time and was installed by the delivery men. Imagine my surprise when I found, as I went to make up the bed, that the mattress I had picked was as hard as a park bench!

I took off the covering, and there it was — a solid block of wood!

I immediately called the store, but was told by the salesman that I would have to speak to the owner, who was not available. Meanwhile, I was sleeping on my living room couch, which was hardly what you'd call restful.

That situation turned out to be my first encounter with Small Claims Court, where, in making out the application for restitution, I was told I would have to have the owner served with a subpoena. Since I was already down in the courts area, I went to the buildings data office, and after a three-hour search, I came up with the information that the owner was none other than the salesman who had sold me the mattress!

Next, I had a friend take a snapshot of the con man as he left the store — with me hiding nearby to point him out. Just in case he had seen my friend taking the picture, I asked another friend to do the serving, since he was able to recognize the owner from the photo.

My friend strolled casually into the store, pretending to be a customer and asking many questions. When a real prospect entered, the salesman handed my friend his card and suggested that he call him when he had made up his mind.

"Oh, would you please write down the model numbers?" my friend asked, handing the salesman/owner a pencil along with the subpoena.

The faker's plea in court was that the trucking company had made an error, but the judge looked at him skeptically and told him to correct that error by refunding the amount I had paid plus the cost of my application to the court.

The store closed a short time later — even before I had a chance to find a bed elsewhere!

Catalogs

My father once told us that one night in the *Follies* when Will Rogers was spinning his rope and making his humorous remarks, a cat walked across the stage behind him. He had not yet gotten to a punch line, so he was mystified by the roar of laughter from the audience. When he turned around and saw the cat, he shooed him off the stage, admonishing, "Get out of here, kitty, this is a monologue, not a catalog."

Daddy had been teasing me and my sisters about our addiction to catalogs. I think we were on every mailing list in the country. I still am, and for a long time after my sister Natalie's death, her husband didn't bother to cancel any of her subscriptions, which arrived almost daily. I think the continuity was comforting.

Buying clothes from a catalog was always easy for me, because if they had my size, I knew whatever I bought would fit — that is, except for sleeves and pants hems. There was only petite for many years — not petite short, and I would have to cut and hem both of those or I would look like Dopey of the Seven Dwarfs. Natalie and Edna always bought separates, because they were a different size on top or on the bottom. Marilyn ordered wildly. I think it was because she enjoyed sending things back even more than actually wearing them! Margie was the only one who preferred buying clothes only from a store, where she could try them on. From catalogs she was much more interested in book bargains or electronics to help her with her home movies.

Ah, but the gadgets! The wonderful little inventions that were so enticing and so inexpensive! It was always a thrill when a package would arrive. I'd often have forgotten what I ordered, so it was like getting a surprise gift in the mail. Some of them were really clever and worked well — especially items for the kitchen, but then there were some whoppers that had no business being advertised.

Because I live in a busy section of midtown Manhattan, there are always people on the street every hour of the day or night. Many a time I would find myself giving an impromptu dinner party the next day, so I would dash out to the market (only one long block away) in the middle of the night to be prepared. My friends worried about my nocturnal trips and encouraged me to buy some form of protection. I don't think pepper spray was legal (or if I purchased it, I would probably think it belonged in a casserole!), so I finally obliged them by ordering what looked in the picture like a little hand grenade. The instructions said in case of an attack to pull the string and a sound would be emitted that could be heard for ten miles around.

There was also a warning not to test this in the house, because it could be deafening! Of course, I could hardly wait to go outside and try it. What came out was a faint hum that wouldn't have disturbed a fly.

And speaking of flies, my son would rather face a lion than any kind of insect. In the summertime he often forgets and opens his window wide, thus inviting flying bugs inside. There in one of my catalogs was what looked like a small tennis racket, which was run on batteries and purported to strike down anything that could be struck midair. I promptly had it sent to him, but when I finally saw it, I could understand why he asked me if I had lost my mind! It was a full-sized racket that was much too heavy to lift, aim and swat at a moment's notice.

Then there are the candy catalogs — the ones that offer cute serving receptacles, like a squirrel to hold nuts or an egg to contain marshmallow eggs. Once again the photos are deceiving. The squirrel will hold barely a mouthful of nuts, and the egg could squeeze about two marshmallows. I have also learned to beware of sending sugar-free chocolates to diabetic friends. They are sweetened with either maltitol or sorbitol, which are harmless if you eat one or two pieces, but disastrous if you gobble up the entire box, which is what diabetics craving sweets are all too liable to do!

I was so disappointed when my "automatic stirrer" arrived, because I found that it worked only with a pot that had no slant and was even on all sides. Most pots slope from the top rim to the pot bottom. However, I was lucky to find another brand that is also run by batteries, but it sits by itself in the pot, stirring away with "no hands, Ma!"

My ex-husband was looking for an inexpensive wristwatch with an alarm, and I found one that had a choice of sounds — a rooster crowing, a bell ringing, a trumpet playing or water rushing. We carefully read the directions and chose the bell, but when we set the time for the alarm, we got the rooster. We turned the alarm off and decided to use it as an ordinary watch, but, come hell or high water, that determined rooster would wake him day or night at the supposedly designated time. He returned it to the company with a strong recommendation that they remove their watches from the catalog or send the rooster to a farm.

When I first got a computer, I ordered a computer desk from an office furniture catalog. Since I have no trouble following manuals, I assembled it myself, although I was concerned that four of the bolts didn't exactly match up with the pre-drilled holes and had to be forced. I went ahead and finished it. Foolish move! I was underneath when it collapsed on top of me, and I had to call my son on my barely reachable phone to come and get me out!

Many catalogs advertise "bonus" gifts, and some of them are really handy. Other ones, however, are so silly that I can't imagine who thinks them up. One was a small pair of scissors shaped like a stork! Another was an umbrella hat — yes, a band that went on your head with a small umbrella attached. All I could think of was Steve Martin's arrow.

Oh, there's UPS with a package! I wonder what I ordered…

The Pen Isn't Always Mightier

I have a very smart friend who is now retired, but even when he was still practicing as a lawyer, he managed to win every contest he entered, and these were no guessing games; they really took a keen mind and writing skills. He acquired everything from household appliances to vacation cruises, but always remained his sweet, unassuming self — justifyiably proud, but never boastful self.

Personally, I almost never see a contest advertised, but I was once intrigued by one involving poetry.

I'm a lyricist, not a poet, but I can write a poetic lyric if it's required by a character in a play. However, it's still a song, not a poem. I've written only three poems in my adult life — one was a eulogy to my sister, one was an emotional response to my beloved granddaughter's moving 3,000 miles away, and the third was about a pair of pigeons, personifying the sadness of loss.

One day I received an email from a publishing company inquiring if I would like to enter a poem in their annual writing contest. My pigeon poem was just sitting on my desk, so I thought "why not?" This is the poem I sent:

EVERYDAY OCCURRENCE

For several years two pigeons shared a ledge across from mine.
I'd see them from my kitchen as they'd coo and mate and dine
On crumbs they'd bring each other like the finest food and wine.
Yesterday as I prepared a meal for longtime friends,
I idly checked my pigeons as I do when daylight ends.
The female fluttered helplessly; she prodded, pecked and tried
To move the frozen male as he lay stiffly on his side.
Today they both have vanished, and I wonder who will mourn.

I ponder nature's cycle from the day that we are born.
For I have also known the depths of grief, but I have sworn
To grasp the happiness at hand and be aware of joy,
As memories are something even time cannot destroy.

Their answer was suspiciously quick in arriving. Although I was not going to receive any remuneration of any kind, they were certain that I would be delighted to be included in their book of collected poems, and they wanted to know how many copies of the leather-bound books I would like to buy for only $30 a piece.

I told them very, very politely what they could do with their books.

Hollywood Hack

Sitting in on an occasional piano lesson of my sister Edna's, I started to play piano myself when I was six. I was thoroughly familiar with the keyboard, but only vaguely aware of the printed music. Still, I began to write my own simple little songs and to play them by ear.

When we moved from New York to California permanently, my folks engaged the music teacher most well known around Hollywood. She had rattled off all the stars' children she had taught and captivated my eager parents with her chic appearance and self-confidence.

I started lessons with great enthusiasm, and she quickly explained what the lines and spaces meant, plus having me tap out the beats for the note values. That was my entire groundwork!

On my second lesson I was given a short piece to play. She put the music on the rack and waited. Totally bewildered, I asked her to play it for me. Listening carefully, I watched her fingers and played back the little song with ease. She was ecstatic at how easy this was going to be.

At every lesson the same process was repeated. She never once insisted that I play straight from the music, or she would have found that I had absolutely no eye/hand coordination and was *never* sight reading. Also, she had managed to get abridged versions of some of the piano classics, so I was playing Beethoven, Chopin, Liszt and Schubert, etc. with great gusto and honest emotion. We never attempted Bach, because I suspect that she couldn't manage fugues herself.

When it came time for group performances, so that the parents could *qvell* over their children's progress, I was always included. The pieces we chose to play were supposed to be memorized, so I didn't need to pretend to read music at those times.

There were other perks supplied by this "teacher," who, by the way, looked more like a refined fortune teller than anything professorial. Every month we would "win" a very small plaster bust of a famous composer, basically to bribe us to practice. I was thrilled with my collection, never giving it a thought that I practiced voluntarily for at least an hour a day — even the dreaded Hanon exercises.

One contrivance I silently refused to adopt was the nickname she had given herself, a cutesy variation of her real name. I simply avoided calling her anything at all.

A few years later I began studying with a true musician, but my sight reading never improved — or even existed.

How different it was when I took typing classes in high school! We were taught the "touch" system from day one, and I could easily keep my eyes on the report I was copying while my fingers flew over the keys. Even after I learned shorthand, I could decipher what I had written while automatically typing it out.

No eye/hand coordination? Apparently that was not my problem. I can still type my music into my computer, but I can't play it back on the piano. To my unbridled joy, the computer will play it back for me, but I'm handicapped when it comes to any live rendition.

What's so sad is that you can't teach *this* old dog new tricks!

Scam Boomerang

Most New Yorkers are friendly and generous. We'll go out of our way to walk a tourist to his destination if he can't figure out what's East or West. We'll also hand out money to someone who is genuinely hungry and in dire straits.

But we're not suckers!

There are scam artists who are so ingenious that it makes me wonder why they can't find a legitimate job. Of course, I'm not talking about folks caught in a deep recession; I'm referring to the times when we've had a stable economy. I have to confess that I've enjoyed playing along and leaving them frustrated, but feeling kindly toward me. It's sort of a hobby to beat them at their own game.

A few years ago I would come across beggars appropriately dressed in rags who would stake out specific blocks for their operation, and since they'd all look well fed and rested, it was easy to assume that they "went to work" each day like everyone else.

Ah, but there were the creative ones! Coming home from work at The Children's Television Workshop one evening, I was approached by a good-looking, neatly dressed, well-spoken young man. Since I live in the theatre district, his opener was to ask me if I was in show business. I gave him a friendly smile and admitted that I was a writer. He immediately launched into his prepared chronicle of how he was a thirty-three-year-old actor getting his first big break. He had garnered a big part in a play that was being produced at the Long Wharf Theatre in Connecticut, but didn't have a new suit or the carfare to get there.

"Oh," I said sympathetically, "have you spoken to Equity about this?"

"No, I just know that it's up to me to be there for rehearsal next week, and I'm to wear a more current style than I own."

"Long Wharf is a reputable theatre, so I think what you should do right away is go to the Equity office with your contract and have them straighten it out."

"I haven't received my contract yet," he continued weakly, realizing that he hadn't found a pigeon, but should give it one last chance.

"That's all the more reason for you to contact Equity right now. You *do* have their address, don't you?"

"Of course," he answered, now desperate to get rid of me. "Thanks for the advice." He hurried off in the opposite direction from the Equity office, which was a mere five blocks away.

Only about two months later I happened to be in the Wall Street area, picking up some legal papers from my lawyer's downtown office. It seems to me that a good con man should develop a reliable memory, but there was my "actor" friend, and he didn't recognize me. His introduction was, "Excuse me, Miss, but do you work on Wall Street?"

"Oh, my goodness," I cried. "Did you lose the job at the Long Wharf? Have you left show business for good? Well, best of luck to you." With that I dropped down into the subway and left him to figure it out.

I have come across only one woman scammer, and she wasn't very successful. She'd stand at the corner of Broadway and 58th Street, dressed in a neat business suit, and try to sell "investments." I guess she didn't realize that her "office" space was a dead giveaway, and she didn't last long.

But the male "businessmen" seemed to flourish. One night I was leaving Lincoln Center after seeing a show, and in the crowd on the street was another well-dressed, handsome young man who would hurry along, stop and look around and then hurry along again, appearing to be very distressed. He didn't approach any couples, but when he found that I was alone, I became his target.

"Pardon me, Miss, but I don't know what to do. My wallet was just stolen with my credit cards and everything else, including my ticket home to Long Island. Could I possibly borrow the fare from you and send you a check as soon as I get home?"

To panhandle for such a small sum almost seemed on the up and up, but I considered the fact that he could have done this with every single person in the crowd.

"Have you reported it to the police?"

"No, I'll miss my train."

"It's more important that you get this on record; they'll see that you get home."

"But I have a job interview in the morning, and this is the last train tonight."

"As I said, the police will either get you home or let you stay at the station house until tomorrow so that you don't miss your interview. There's a cop right over there. Ask him where the nearest police station is."

Trying to continue to look desperate and not show that he was enormously annoyed at having wasted his time with me, he quickly crossed the street — away from where the policeman stood.

About a month later, I had once again attended a concert at Lincoln Center, and who should be mingling in the exiting crowd but the lost soul from Long Island. As he foolishly focused on me, I exclaimed, "Oh, you poor dear man! You never did get home to Long Island. Have you moved to Manhattan?"

Shipping and Manhandling

When I was a little girl in New York, I was fascinated by the electricity in the air in the winter. My father had taught me the tricks of rubbing a balloon or a playing card vigorously on the carpet and then having it stick to the wall by itself.

My sisters added more fun by getting under the covers with me at bedtime and rubbing our toes briskly back and forth on the sheets, causing little sparks to light up. Later on, I continued this with my daughter and then with *her* daughter. We pretended we had caught a shooting star.

Somehow this didn't work in California. It must be a different climate.

Now here I am an adult in New York, and the winter electricity is no longer a game. No matter how hard I brush my hair or how quickly I try to take away the brush, my hair wants to go with it and ends up standing straight out from my head. This necessitates the use of hairspray, which leaves my hair either sticky or stiff.

I was delighted when I saw an ad for a spray that *guaranteed* just to tame hair, not re-texture it. "Send for a free sample," they invited, so I did. My clue should have been that they also required my credit card number (to cover the shipping and handling).

The phrase "shipping and handling" always conjures up a silly picture in my mind anyway, as I see the packer romantically fondling the inanimate object before putting it into a box.

Remember when you could go into a store and actually purchase a sample, bring it home by yourself, try it out and decide whether you wanted to go back and buy the full size? As a teenager I ended up with an entire drawer full of tiny lipsticks in various shades!

Recently it took three incidents for me to catch on to the latest scams. During the month that follows the "free trial," you are sent a large box or bag filled with more of the company's products, and your credit card is charged accordingly.

This is accompanied by a brochure in large print stating the virtues of the products, and in small print you are advised to return the merchandise within a short period of time or not only will you be billed (which you already have been on your credit card) for what was delivered, but you will receive more of the same and be billed every month!

With the return and your request to cancel your account, you are finally off the hook, but the cost of the return shipping is not refunded.

The latest one (and the last time I will ever be this gullible) had the nerve to put on their website a button for a "quick cancel." Their explanation was that instead of the $39.95 they had charged me (I never got that second package at all, by the way), they would charge me only $13.41, and I could keep the merchandise!

I have returned the sample and informed my credit card company, which is extremely reliable in removing unsolicited charges.

My hair is rather stiff, but very neat.

Not A Clue

While I was still making the rounds with my music, I would take various writing assignments and would do either complete research or use some knowledge of my own and supplement it.

One time I was called upon to write an article about an undergraduate of a psychoanalytical institute. I was to go to him for therapy and evaluate his performance. He, of course, was not informed of the arrangement, which, in a way, I thought was rather sneaky.

His office was a short subway ride from my apartment, and the exit was practically at the door of the building. Easy to get to on time.

On Day One he met me at his office door and shook hands. He was a young man with red hair, the only distinguishing feature of his totally nondescript appearance.

We entered into a very dark room. He had drawn the shades, and the only light was from the lamp on his desk. Because I'm a night owl and stay up until all hours, I can easily take a nap during the day if I find myself horizontal and reasonably comfortable. I explained this to the would-be therapist, announcing that I would therefore prefer to sit in the chair rather than lie on the couch.

"Do you have trouble trusting men?" he asked.

At first I was confused, because I couldn't associate this utterly bland creature with lust. I repeated my reason for sitting in the chair unless he wanted to risk my falling sound asleep and missing the entire session.

Silence.

"I'd like to start with free association. If I say a word, would you please answer with the first word that comes into your mind?"

"Okay."

"Black/white; day/night; summer/winter; love/hate; hot/cold — all the usual responses I'd heard so many times.

Silence.

"What activities do you enjoy?"

"Reading, cooking, sewing, writing, watching movies and shows and participating in politics."

"In that order?"

"No, pick what you want from Column A or Column B."

No response. This was my first confirmation that he had no sense of humor.

The rest of the session was equally dull, but I showed up the following week to find that we were both in the elevator. As we entered his dismal office, he asked, "What did you think when you saw me in the elevator?"

"I figured we were both going to the same place at the same time."

Another nonproductive session.

The following week, in the dim, dim light, I thought I saw the beginning of a beard — hard to tell on a redhead in a semi-dark room.

"Are you growing a beard?"

He was overjoyed (well, not overjoyed exactly, more pleased) that he thought he had found a basis for bonding or whatever.

"Do you like beards?"

"Yes, my son has one, and it's very becoming."

Silence.

As we reached the ground floor, someone brought him his dog, a large jolly police dog, which I assume had been tied up awaiting his return. I patted the dog's head, and he licked my hand.

Naturally, the following session opened with "Do you like dogs?"

"Very much, and yours is such a nice, friendly dog."

"What did you think when you saw my dog?"

"That yours is such a nice, friendly dog."

Silence.

After the next session we found ourselves on the same subway. His question was true to form the following week. "What did you think when you saw me on the subway?"

"I figured we were going uptown, and if one of us wanted to go downtown, that person was on the wrong subway."

I had had enough and no longer cared whether my article would be acceptable. I told the therapist that I was discontinuing our sessions, because I felt we were wasting a great deal of time. He said he thought we should have a session to discuss my decision.

"That's what we're doing, discussing my decision, and this *is* the final session. I want to wish you the best of luck."

"So should I go f**k myself?" he suddenly shouted loudly.

"Yes," I agreed, shocked by his outburst, but glad for him that there was indeed a living person inside that cardboard cutout.

With that, I left his shadowy room and his half-grown beard and got on the uptown subway.

I do hope he chose another profession.

The Eyes Have It

When I was nine, my family moved to California permanently, and I was heartbroken, resolving to return home to New York as soon as I was old enough. I did just that.

Not having left with any rancor or rebelliousness, I stayed in close touch, speaking to my folks on the phone every Friday night and delighted when either they or any of my sisters came for a visit.

I did, however, create my own "family" of friends — the man who eventually became my husband, a witty friend of his who lived in the same building, a nice Iowan couple with two little children (they never did become typical New Yorkers, but remained bewildered for as long as I could remember), a young man who disappeared every summer, but who returned in the winter with apparently enough funds so that he could enjoy everything the city had to offer, and the "odd couple," a woman much, much older than the rest of us, who never gave her age, but who slipped now and then with references to events and places before our time, and her young roommate, who ended up paying most of their bills.

When my own roommate got homesick for California and returned there, I needed another friend to share the rent. The only one available was not one, but two — the older and younger women. It was then that I got the story of their alliance.

The younger woman had come from a home with a stern, overbearing mother, who was strict about her daughter's sticking to her every rule. Because the girl could sing and dance a little, she escaped by joining the USO and going overseas. When she returned, she answered an ad to share an apartment with another woman, who happened to be old enough to be her mother.

What a combination! Here was the kind, supportive, indulgent mother the girl had always wished for, and the older woman, who was a great cook and made all their meals, never had to feel guilty about not paying her share of anything while looking for acting jobs for herself. She was not a very good actress, but happened to be an excellent director, so every summer she was hired to direct high-school kids at a drama camp.

Come fall and she'd spend almost every day in the park, writing the great American play that somehow never got finished. She would pick up various people and convince them and herself that she was their muse, no matter what field of the arts they pursued. One beautiful young Irishman wrote poetry, and it didn't bother her a bit that none of it made any sense. He came from a wealthy family, who found it necessary to have him committed now and then for his odd behavior — like appearing in the park stark naked and trying to make love to a tree.

His younger brother, however, did have talent, and I wrote the music to one of his lyrics. The song was immediately picked up by a publisher, who wanted to sign us to a contract. Because he was still underage, his father refused to let him sign the contract — probably because he felt it was much safer to train him to enter the family business.

Greenwich Village was at that time considered a haven for anyone in the arts. Rents were low, and there were many open-air markets for fruits and vegetables. The regular markets always had sales on meat, fish and chicken. Also, everyone was eager to help everyone else. Actresses posed free for artists; musicians sang and played auditions for composers out of nothing more than friendship; those who were secretaries by day typed playwrights' scripts at night.

A newcomer to the "muse's" coterie was a charming photographer who looked astonishingly like Blair Underwood (of days to come). The first thing he said upon meeting me was that I had such beautiful eyes he would like to photograph them. In no way did I consider this to be a pick-up line, because I had been told flattering things about my eyes from the time I first put on make-up in high school! We set a time for me to come to his studio.

Climbing the two flights to his loft, where he also lived, I found a room full of his excellent photographs and all kinds of camera equipment and lights. He was at his butcher block next to four burners, busy cutting up meat and vegetables with a large knife for a stew he was making.

"I'll be with you in a minute," he said. "I got a late start."

While I watched him, I noticed that two fingers were missing, and I'm afraid I couldn't resist.

"Don't you run out of fingers?"

He laughed good-naturedly and explained that actually he had been studying the violin while earning a living in a factory. There was an accident, and that was the end of his dreams of being a violinist.

"When I recovered, I took up photography, because I had reasoned that a dissonant chord sounds irritating to the ear, but when it's part of a symphony, it adds to the texture of the entire piece, and changing my career goal was part of the symphony of my life."

I never forgot that insightful approach to living.

When he finished browning the meat and put everything into the pot for simmering, he apologized for the delay and posed me on his sofa. He then began to set up the lights and peer through his camera.

"Would you please remove your blouse? I'd like to take a portrait shot which would include bare shoulders."

I was wearing an opaque bra similar to the top of a two-piece bathing suit, so I felt no embarrassment in complying.

"Oh, the straps are in the way," he said. "Maybe you'd better remove the bra, too."

"I can lower the straps if you'll give me something to tuck into my bra."

He came over and put his arm around me. "Let's see," he said.

Now, if this sounds like the beginning of an episode of *Law and Order, Special Victims Unit*, I can put your mind at ease. There was no rape, no murder and no violence whatsoever. I found him immensely attractive, but I was in no way ready for a casual physical relationship. He understood this, took the pictures without any further disrobing and promised to send me prints when they were completed. He did. We had become friends.

A Midsummer Night's Scheme

I was on my first paid vacation from my secretarial job in New York and visiting my folks in California when I got a call from my friend-who-thought-she-was-a-muse in New York informing me that she had gone into partnership with an experienced young man who was starting up a regional theatrical company. They were looking for apprentices for the summer — acting jobs that provided room and board, but no pay. She wondered if I'd be interested in playing the ingénue comedy parts.

Would I? I jumped at the chance on was on the next plane home, memorizing my first part on the plane. When I arrived in New York, she told me we would all be going to Rochester together. No, not Rochester, New York, but Rochester, New Hampshire. We were to play in an old opera house there and stay in the rooming house across the street, which also provided the meals, family style.

There was a married couple who were to manage the books and the box office, a good-looking leading man, a pretty leading lady, a young character actor who was to play opposite me in the comedies and another young girl who was to play all the straight ingénue parts.

The leading man and the young character actor roomed together; the pretty leading lady and I were roommates; the young ingénue was assigned to a room with our "muse," and the married couple, of course, had their own room.

Everything seemed on the up and up except for a few peculiarities, such as my roommate's confiding to me that she had a boyfriend on Mars, and they were engaged to be married as soon as his rocket trip was booked.

We played one show at night and rehearsed the next one during the day. Even Elliot Norton, the biggest Boston critic, gave me a rave review, which, unfortunately, I didn't know what to do with and had no idea how to audition when I did get back to New York.

Now, getting back to New York was the major problem. The "experienced young man" with whom our "muse" had gone into partnership had absconded with *all* the money from the box office and treasury box and had disappeared without a trace.

Fortunately, for me, I had saved enough money from my job (and had brought it with me) to buy a train ticket home, but most of the cast was left stranded. The two male actors pooled what they had and scraped by, and the married couple was able to get an advance from a job they had been promised in New York. The "muse" wrote to her roommate in New York to send her the money, and the young ingénue simply married a local guy and settled down there!

Years later the instigator was found; he had opened another company legitimately, but it failed, and once again he was gone.

So was I — from acting. I found writing music and raising kids was much more fulfilling, and I guess I'm not ham enough to need to be seen.

A House Is Not A Home

The first year my husband and I were married was the last year my folks lived in the large house where we had all lived until two of my sisters got married, one got her own apartment and two of us moved back to New York. Since they were going to move into a much smaller house with no stairs to climb, no swimming pool to maintain and a minimum staff, they invited us to spend the summer with them in the "big house," as it was called, before their new home was ready.

We had a wonderful summer — even made a home movie written, directed and filmed by my sister Margie. As with all of her movies, it was silent, inasmuch as there was no sound camera available then for home use, but the titles she wrote for the "spoken" dialogue were hilarious.

On our next trip, we brought along an addition — baby Brian, and we stayed at my sister Edna's house. When Amanda came along, we spent that summer at my sister Natalie's house, but from then on, it was a different rented apartment every summer.

We had no idea what a task this was for Margie and Natalie. *No one* wanted to rent for just three months, and furnished apartments were even harder to find. Not only was it heartbreaking to have to board our cat (*absolutely no pets*), but *no children* was also the order of the day. Did they expect us to board them also?

Although the rents were not exorbitant, the owners managed to tack on extra fees for anything they could think of.

One apartment looked exactly like the Bates Motel — especially the shower. It didn't bother the kids, but my husband and I became very nervous bathers, and there was a charge for water over a certain amount (we never knew what amount or who calculated it).

Then there was the large apartment on the Sunset Strip (Sunset Blvd. just before entering Hollywood from Beverly Hills). The building stood right between two bars and across the street from a "club" known for its tough customers, who would spill out onto the street for fistfights. To add to its charm, all the side streets coming down from the hills led straight into Sunset Blvd. with no traffic signals whatsoever. There was no air conditioning, so we had to leave our windows open, and if we didn't hear the vindictive obscenities from the brawlers across the street, we would hear the screech of brakes as a driver would try to make it onto the boulevard from the hills before the next car would come speeding by. The indifferent answer my husband got when he went to the police station to inquire about traffic signals at those points was, "Yeah, we put 'em up after the third fatal accident."

Ah, then there was the tall blonde lady with the twisted neck! Her head was permanently facing her left shoulder, but it certainly didn't hinder her bargaining powers. She had no garage, and I had borrowed a car for the summer and had to do something with it at night, because parking on the street was not allowed. She managed to find someone at the end of the block who was going away for the summer, so she charged us to use that person's parking space in their garage.

If we came home after 9PM, I would drop off my husband and kids and put the car away, but on the way back up the block the click of my heels on the sidewalk would cause every window to light up in every building. As New Yorkers, we're used to walking everywhere, but apparently it's just not done in the residential sections of Beverly Hills.

One late afternoon my husband picked up our clothes from the cleaner's and was walking back to the apartment, when he was stopped by the police and questioned. We didn't have credit cards then, and he hadn't yet learned to drive, so he didn't have a license or anything else for identification. His New York library card wasn't of any use, but when he pulled out his Screen Actors Guild card, it worked like magic. Hooray for Hollywood!

Those were the days when all apartment buildings were painted either dusty rose or Nile green — why I don't know, because so many of the buildings were erected before Technicolor. Maybe those awful colors actually slowed down the process of anyone even wanting to try to perfect it. They were also all stucco. In one apartment we had carefully put the chain on the lock as we were getting ready for bed, but one of my sisters came over, knocked on the door, figured we didn't hear her and turned the knob. The door opened all right, because the entire lock fell out of the stucco wall, and the landlord wanted to charge us for a new lock.

Every summer my sister Edna would give a "swap" party at her house in Malibu, which she had designed herself, and it was absolutely beautiful.

The entrance was right on the Pacific Coast Highway, and the door opened on a very large living room to the side of which was a tiny bedroom and bath and next to that a kitchen furnished with professional appliances. The entire back wall was glass and faced the ocean. She relished her solo activities, like long walks on the beach, reading, writing, painting and listening to jazz, but she also had many friends and enjoyed giving marvelous and unusual parties.

For the swap, the rule was that a person or couple was to bring along either a large tablecloth or blanket and set up their display in whatever part of the room they had staked out. There could be as many or as few items as they wished, but everything had to be from home, either brand new or in excellent condition. You could also give a voucher for a one-time service, such as a home-cooked dinner for six, a personal car wash or babysitting. Edna provided the buffet and drinks, which were available all evening.

Inasmuch as my husband and I were visiting from New York, we had no items to trade, and trading was done with great seriousness. If one person had something you wanted, but you didn't have anything they wanted, you could in all likelihood exchange with someone else to acquire the desirable item and then barter for the thing you wanted in the first place. Every year we would raid my folks' store room, which was filled with gifts and other articles that they didn't know how to get rid of. We'd always arrive with the same old ugly chartreuse lazy susan, a dinner gong and an old-fashioned dressing table set consisting of a brush, a comb and a hand mirror, lavishly painted in art deco style.

There was nothing left to do but to "scam it," so we bought a bottle of champagne, pretending it had been given to us, and we finally made our entrance into the marketplace!

South of The Border

Being the youngest in the family by six years, my bedtime came long before the others. After Winnie, my nanny, would tuck me in for the night, Mother would send Daddy upstairs to perform the good night ceremony.

He'd lie on the side of my bed and recite the various fairy tales he knew, but when I didn't drift off, he'd give a mock command.

"The first one who laughs goes to Mexico."

I had no idea where or what Mexico was, but I loved the game.

Then he'd say something silly, and I'd giggle.

"Oh, there you go!" he'd announce. Of course, I'd beg for another chance, so once again he'd say something silly, and once again I'd giggle.

"That does it!" he'd cry, and I'd end up getting several more chances.

When my giggles were beginning to get muffled, he'd conclude, "That's the very end! I'm going downstairs to book your ticket!"

He'd kiss me goodnight, make sure I was safely tucked in and go downstairs to join the rest of the family.

I'd go to sleep with the comfort of the smell of his hair tonic on my pillow and the hum of the family noise downstairs.

Getting A Ticket

Does life mirror art? Yes, in some cases. My father had made a short with the above title and acted it out shamelessly right in front of me one day!

He had taken me to an afternoon movie, which had gotten out just about dinner time, and he was hurrying home to be at the dinner table on time.

Fortunately, there weren't many other cars on Sunset Boulevard that day, and he was paying no attention to the speed limit while lecturing me about safe driving and bragging that he had never gotten a ticket.

I wasn't surprised when we heard the siren and the command to "pull over." The officer was delighted to meet the popular star, but he was about to make out the ticket anyway, when my father went into a very funny routine, involving the cop as straight man whenever possible.

By the time he finished, the policeman was laughing so hard that he waved us away *sans* ticket. "So *that's* how you never got a ticket," I remarked. He winked at me and said, "Don't try it!"

I did get away with it, but it certainly wasn't on purpose. I had been visiting Winnie several miles away when I got a call from my sister Margie, informing me that my idol, Danny Kaye, was actually at our house and I would at last have a chance to meet him.

"I don't know how long he'll be here, but don't drive too fast," she warned.

I was doing about 90, when a cop stopped me. He bawled me out and was about to write up the ticket when I burst into tears. He felt so sorry for me that he said, since it was my first offense, he would let me off with a warning. I thanked him profusely and proceeded on my way. Little did he know that the tears were not about getting a ticket, but possibly not getting home in time to meet Danny Kaye.

At Your Service

Many years ago, my son had a friend who was trying to establish his small recording studio. He would lure clients in by giving talented but yet unknown singers free studio time and then offer to get the demos to the various record producers.

His skill at promotion was incredible, and he did keep his promises. However, it was still a one-man operation, which he kept cleverly hidden from those he was approaching.

If a producer agreed to listen to a tape, there would usually be a request that he receive it immediately — especially on a Friday, so that he could play it in his car on his way to his weekend retreat.

From taking my own cassettes around to producers and hearing that same old story, I finally asked one of them what he would do if he didn't have a car — rent one just to listen to a tape he could hear in his office?

Anyway, the ambitious young man with the studio would tell the producer that he was sending the tape over by messenger, at which point he would turn on his phone machine, sling his carrier bag over his shoulder and hop on his bike, heading for the producer's mailroom, where he would mark the package URGENT — IMMEDIATE DELIVERY REQUESTED and sign in with the name of a fictitious messenger service.

It worked, but he couldn't be responsible for the producer's taste in singers. Those who did get noticed remained loyal to him, and eventually he did indeed have a full staff, a well-equipped studio and access to a messenger service.

Innocent Bystander

My father laughed when recalling his inadvertent participation in a scam when he was a young boy. To avoid getting beaten up by the bullies in his neighborhood, he'd entertain them and make them laugh, and he mistakenly assumed that they had become his friends — especially when they would suggest street corners where he might draw a crowd and earn some coins. Little did he know that as soon as he'd start singing, his "friends" would start picking pockets. If he didn't acquire many pennies and nickels, his "agents" would occasionally hand him 50¢, which bound him to them in gratitude.

A Bit O' Blarney

Winnie had long since changed from the naïve little farm girl who came to stay with us at twenty-two from the emerald isle. She still had her brogue, but was hip to everything that went on and used to all the show-business pranks and idiosyncrasies.

Every summer some friends or relatives from Ireland would spend their vacations visiting America, and all of them were movie struck and thrilled that Winnie actually lived in the land of make believe.

Of course, they were dying to see the movie stars' homes, but Winnie would save them the cost of the bus tour and take them around herself. Every time she'd pass a particularly beautiful mansion, she'd announce the name of the celebrity who lived there and relate a kindly little anecdote about the star, neither of which had any basis in truth!

If by chance they had already bought postcards depicting the actual residences, she'd confide that they had just moved, making sure that her travelogue ended right near a lovely place for lunch. Every now and then she'd burst out with "Oh, there's so-and-so!" but when they all looked in the same direction and saw no one vaguely recognizable, she'd murmur, "Oh, I guess you just missed him; he was on his way out the door."

After buying a multitude of souvenirs at many of the tourist traps, the visitors would return to Ireland, thanking Winnie profusely and eager to share their adventures with their home companions.

I assume Winnie went to confession after telling such tall tales, but it's my guess that the reprimand barely rated a Hail Mary!

Just Say No

My father was a health nut. He read non-fiction books and all newspapers thoroughly every day, and if there was an article about foods that were good for you, he'd order them by the case and insist that we consume them. He switched us from white bread to whole wheat and poured us glass after glass of carrot juice (good for eyesight, although none of us wore glasses), but I simply wouldn't cooperate when it came to vegetables — I'd eat them, but I wouldn't drink them.

He was indeed energetic and usually healthy himself, and it's sad that the deli sandwiches and anything chocolate that he enjoyed the most probably were the things that upped his cholesterol and eventually led to his heart attack.

Having been dubbed "The Apostle of Pep," he certainly lived up to it in movies and on stage, but at home he was verbally, rather than physically, funny and didn't go around popping his eyes or jumping up and down. His exercise included a lot of brisk walking, and whenever he got a chance, he'd play ping pong, as both he and my sister Natalie were champions.

One night he was playing gin rummy with his pal Georgie Jessel; and his business manager, Jack Crandall, also an old friend, was kibitzing. They were sitting around with their sleeves rolled up and their shirt buttons open. When my father excused himself to go to the bathroom, Georgie turned to Jack and said with a sigh, "It's such a shame about Eddie."

"What do you mean?"

"His drug addiction, of course."

"He has an *addiction*?"

"Well, just watch. He'll come out of that bathroom all hopped up and ready to play all night. He probably needed a fix."

Jack ran to the bathroom and pounded on the door.

"LET ME IN!"

My father assumed Jack needed the bathroom in a hurry, so he opened the door while drying his hands. Jack grabbed the towel and shook it.

"Stop it, Eddie. Stop it right now!"

"Stop drying my hands?"

"You know what I mean. Think of Ida. Think of the girls."

"They can dry their own hands."

Jack clutched my father's arms, checking for needle marks.

"What pills did you take?"

"Well, let's see — my vitamins and some extra Vitamin C, and…"

"*You know what I mean*! Georgie, come here."

Jack flung open the bathroom door, and there was Georgie, convulsed with laughter and sputtering to his friend about the gag he had pulled.

Fiddler
On A Hot Tin Roof

Many years ago I used to be able to travel to see my friends and relatives anywhere out of town that they were playing: my daughter, Amanda Abel, in Boston and Los Angeles, my brother-in-law, Robert Clary, in Long Island, Boston, St. Louis and Kansas City, my friend Caroline Durham in New Jersey and my friend Ted Thurston in Philadelphia and almost in Wantagh, New York.

I say "almost" because of the bizarre circumstances leading up to his performance. I had never seen *Fiddler on the Roof*, and Ted was playing the second lead at the Jones Beach outdoor theatre. In his jolly bass baritone voice, he called me at the Children's Television Workshop and said he'd pick me up after work and we'd drive out to Wantagh together.

When I mentioned that the weather forecast was for heavy rain, he said, with his usual guffaw, "Oh, they always say that!" Therefore I was standing outside my office building when he drove up. As we were leaving the city, it began to get darker and darker, but he still insisted that there was nothing to worry about.

Suddenly, we could see not far ahead of us a big black funnel, twisting and turning and headed right for us. "Auntie Em! Oh, Auntie Em!" we both cried jokingly. But this was not *The Wizard of Oz*. The twister hit us directly and moved on. We were not airborne, but the torrents of rain and hail were so paralyzing that all we could do was stop the car and turn off the motor.

We sat there for about half an hour until the rain actually stopped and the sun came out. "Well, I guess there won't be a performance tonight," I assumed.

"I have to get out there anyway," Ted answered. "It's an Equity rule. Only the stage manager can cancel a performance."

So on we went over the slippery wet highway. Of course, at this hour, the sun wasn't very strong. Nothing was drying up. When we reached the theatre, the huge parking lot was empty of cars but filled with puddles. I couldn't wait for Ted in the audience, because the seats were drenched.

When I came backstage, I heard him ask the stage manager if they were really going to have a performance, and the answer was that he was to get into his costume and makeup immediately.

What a show for preparation! The costume was big and bulky, and the makeup required a long and painstaking application — including the adherence of a beard. The transformation was so great that when Ted came out of his dressing room, I almost didn't recognize him!

Everyone stood around looking at each other for about ten minutes. Then came the announcement over the loudspeaker:

"Attention: tonight's performance has been canceled due to weather conditions."

Brown Bagging It

Jean Bedini and Roy Arthur were a successful vaudeville team known for both elegant style and lowdown humor, plus expert juggling. The dapper Mr. Bedini was basically the star, while Roy Arthur, known as Bunky, played in blackface — carrying on and off the plates, bottles and whatever else was being juggled.

As the act expanded, they felt that they needed an assistant to do the leg work, and they hired my father, a young kid hoping to be in show business but needing a steady salary. He would occasionally make a wisecrack as he exited, and the laughs he got were getting bigger than the entire act.

Mr. Bedini's nose was out of joint at the attention being taken away from him, but Bunky saw the possibilities for the sassy kid and took him under his wing, becoming his father figure and protector.

Vaudeville was on its way out as light opera and early musicals were on their way in, and my father's star rose as Bunky's dimmed. They finally lost touch, but one night, many years later, my father and one of my sisters were riding in a cab to the theatre.

Suddenly, Daddy shouted, "Stop the cab and wait for me!" He had spotted Bunky on the street, looking extremely down and out, and he ran up to him. After giving him a hearty embrace, he asked breathlessly, "Bunky, where have you been? I've been looking all over for you. I have a job for you. Are you available?"

Bunky nodded, confused but eager. "Here's my number at the hotel," my father said, fishing a scrap of paper out of his pocket. "Call me tomorrow and I'll tell you all about it."

As he hopped back into the cab, my sister asked, "What job?"

"I don't know, but I'll think of one by tomorrow."

That was how Bunky came into our lives for the rest of his. We never knew exactly what Bunky did, but he always managed to keep busy. His wife became one of my father's secretaries, and they were able to put their son through college.

At Daddy's radio shows, when he'd come out to warm up the audience before he went on the air, it was Bunky who would start the applause. If my sister Margie needed an actor for a scene in one of her home movies, Bunky would appear as that character. Plane tickets? Bunky arranged it. Theatre tickets? Bunky acquired the best seats. Thank you flowers to last night's hostess? A beautiful arrangement would arrive right on time.

One day, when Daddy was working in a movie in Burbank, he suddenly needed a great deal of cash for gifts for the cast, so he called his bank and instructed them to release it to Bunky. Within an hour Bunky arrived on the set in a shabby coat and carrying two shopping bags with celery stalks sticking out of one and a very large loaf of bread sticking out of the other.

"What's the matter, Bunky? You look terrible! And what is all this stuff?"

Bunky put down the bags, dropped the coat and went into the bathroom to wash the "age" makeup off his face.

"Eddie, I didn't dare walk around with all that money, and I didn't think it was wise to take a cab, so I did a little shopping at a thrift store and a market and put on some makeup in the gas station bathroom. I got on the next bus to Burbank, and I knew I was safe, because no one wanted to get near me or even look into my bags. Oh, by the way, that's where the money is."

Bunky still knew how to juggle.

At Odds With Nature

When I was a child, I loved playing in Central Park. I really believed all the myths about the dryads and searched every day to see if I could find the twig that would open the tree's lock and free one. I never paid much attention to the flowers, but I did love climbing the rocks and finding little "caves."

When my family moved to California, I was overwhelmed by the well-kept green lawns and carefully created flower beds, but by the time I graduated high school, I had had enough and returned to New York — eventually to raise my own family.

Every sunny day I was back in Central Park, only now I wasn't exploring trees, but sitting on a bench in a playground, while my kids played with their friends. It was a lovely time for me to socialize as well, because the other mothers were interesting people, and our discussions were about books, movies, plays and politics — not about diapers and baby food.

When my kids were 12 and 15, I got a divorce, but their father moved to an apartment only five blocks away, ostensibly so that they could see him whenever they wanted.

He had decorated the apartment in which we were still living and was now busy decorating his own place. The opposite of my indifference to plants and flowers, he loved cultivating them. At one time, early in our marriage, he had followed the popular trend to put toothpicks in a sweet potato and place it in water to grow. He was planning to have the resulting vine grow around the molding of our living room ceiling, but it surprised him by growing straight up and up and up, and we were convinced that it was Jack's beanstalk.

In his own new apartment, he decided to eschew draperies and place tiers of plants against the windows. Of course, this did not block out the windows totally, and he could be seen from the building right across the street. He had also heard that it was beneficial to talk to your plants to ensure their friendly environment. He did not put an air conditioner in the living room window, so as not to freeze the foliage, but he did have one in his bedroom, where he could take refuge on really hot summer days.

One day he came home from working on a commercial art job, and he was so overheated that all he could think about was getting into the shower and then relaxing in the air-conditioned room. He stripped off his clothes, piece by piece, but by the time he was naked, he remembered that he was supposed to talk to his plants. As he greeted each one, he saw an old woman from across the street staring at him in horror, assuming, he figured, that he had a sexual relationship with his greenery. He dropped to the floor and crawled into his bedroom, hoping the old lady had decided to move.

When my kids grew up, my son stayed in the old apartment and my daughter married and moved to Queens. In the course of time she, too, had a little girl, and my grandchild would often stay with me on weekends. There I was back in Central Park, watching her climb the same rocks I had climbed and riding the same carousel.

I still had no interest in flowers, however, and had obviously passed this along to my son. When his father was going away for the weekend, he asked him to water his plants and to be sure *not to miss even one*.

Brian dutifully followed his instructions, but when his father returned the next night, he found a big puddle of water on his kitchen floor. Brian had no explanation, but his father figured it out. There was a big plastic sunflower on the wall that held a note pad for shopping lists, and Brian had watered the sunflower, too.

Those Who Can't...

One of the greatest scams perpetrated on the public began centuries ago: professional criticism. I think it started with "learned" men dictating to the "unschooled" what plays or music or works of art were "worthy" of attention. Of course then, as now, the "common man" would still choose from his own taste in the long run.

I remember when New York had several "important" newspapers, and a rave from at least two could guarantee the success of a play or musical. This was assumed to be a "service," since reading negative reviews would supposedly save your hard-earned cash from being wasted on an unpleasant evening in the theatre or at the movies.

Theatre tickets were not that big an investment when I first moved into the theatre district, a few short blocks from the TKTS tent. I caught on quickly to go to the half-price booth at the last minute, and I was always able to get a single ticket to a preview. Often I would run into my friend Arthur Siegel in the theatre, because he and I wanted to see just about everything, and he used the same system I did. Every now and then we had a special treat when we got to see a sketch or musical number that was cut once the revue opened, even though it was very entertaining, but made the show too long.

Once the show opened, we'd eagerly read the reviews to see if we agreed or not. All too often a really interesting and well-acted drama would be wiped out practically overnight. Musicals, even ones we didn't like, usually had some kind of run.

That's when I stopped reading reviews altogether. We had one critic, an imbiber, who slept soundly through every show, but that didn't stop him from reviewing it, and then there was the snob who preferred opera to musicals and therefore belittled the latter, even including nasty comments about cast members who didn't please his eye. I was sorry to read what the one known to be an academic had to say, because he was highly intelligent, but so analytical that he often missed the point of a show that was meant to be a spoof on other shows of its genre.

I always wished that only the cast and creative crew would be listed, plus a few sentences covering the subject matter, but not giving away the plot. That would certainly have been sufficient. Other people's opinions are stimulating, but only after I've formed my own.

At home we had a running disagreement with my father, because none of us found a very famous leading man to be in the least bit appealing, and my father would keep repeating that he was the #1 box-office draw, so we had to be wrong! We'd then shout that it was our *opinion*, and it didn't matter how famous he was. My sisters and I usually agreed on the same types of men on the screen, but fortunately never in our personal lives! However, no man or woman I ever knew didn't agree that the most attractive man of all time was Cary Grant. And to think that my father had turned him down for the romantic lead in *The Kid from Spain* because he had never heard of him at that time! Many years later I remember standing behind him in the bank one day and marveling that even the back of his neck was handsome!

That's one person about whom no critics were ever in doubt. It was gratifying to find that they appreciated his dramatic acting as much as his comedy, although I'm not so sure the public did.

The worthwhile thing about book reviews is that you can at least get an inkling of what to expect, which you certainly can't by "judging a book by its cover." The blurbs, of course, will quote partial sentences that are all hyperbolic, to say the least. This is like the one-word theatre "raves" for a show that is about to close.

Calling A Spade A Spade

Originally this phrase came from the Greek and meant what it still means: to speak honestly and not euphemistically. During the Civil War, the word "spade" became a derogatory name for a black person — not because of the color of the playing card, but because of the menial work he did digging with a spade.

Euphemisms annoy the daylights out of me. Calling a retarded child "retarded" instead of "mentally challenged" or "special" is not a slur in any way. "Retarded" simply means "slowed down," which is what has happened to the child's brain.

I myself was crippled by a mugger, which has left me "handicapped," or just plain "crippled," not "physically challenged," although every day it's a struggle to meet the various obstacles.

What I find most irritating is the use of all the terms that designate the old or elderly. "Senior" is okay, because it's a short neat word that helps to indicate a category with many legal concerns. But I draw the line at being referred to in any way as "silver." And for hordes of us, these are not "the golden years."

My ex-husband turned sixty-five eight years before I did, but since we were still friends, he'd pass along any information he thought I might eventually find helpful.

One of those things was a "Silver Saver Book." It was filled with discount coupons of no more than 5% off just about anything we'd probably never buy, and it was specific about the coupon accompanying cash.

Our favorite was the coupon for cremation. Now, exactly when were you supposed to present the coupon — on your way into the oven?

Petty Politics

When did race labels become such an issue? When I was in grammar school, we were taught that there were four distinct races: black, white, red and yellow. This always sounded to me like something from my box of crayons, because the "black" people I knew were brown; the "white" people were sort of beige or maybe pink; and I had never seen anyone who was either yellow or red. It's not that I had never met an Asian person or a "Native American," but neither one looked yellow or red.

Black people were called Negroid then, and I thought it was very wise to change that to "Black," because the word was too close to the pejorative "nigger."

"Native American" makes more sense than "Indian," because it distinguishes between a group that was named incorrectly in the first place and the people actually native to India.

But why are the labels, old and new, necessary? I can understand the information being vital for a birth certificate or a driver's license, but I don't know any other practical use. I didn't even know all the bad words for Latinos until I saw John Leguizamo's first hilarious one-man show.

I have never heard a black friend or acquaintance born in this country call him or herself an "African American," but my grandson-in-law really could. He was born on the island of Mauritius and now lives in California. However, he was raised in London, so doesn't that make him an "African British American"? Now, really, can you consider this with a straight face? Actually, his skin is a lovely gold color, which he explained is a throwback to the Creole, because of the early intermarriage of the French with the natives of Mauritius.

Both my great grandchildren are as white as my granddaughter, and my grandson-in-law laughingly told me that one day, when he took the first baby to the park and forgot to bring a bottle, he decided to run all the way home to feed the screaming infant. As he wildly pushed the carriage (or "pram" as he would call it) at top speed, he saw several people looking at him with worried expressions. "They must have been thinking 'Ooh, that black man is running away with that white baby!'" he joked.

When I was young and single, and I would be "fixed up" with a blind date, the young man would sometimes ask if I was Greek or Italian because of my olive skin and black hair. Usually, I could tell what they were getting at, and I'd answer, "No, just plain old New York Jewish." I don't know why there was always a question as to whether Jewish was a race or a religion. Of course it's a race — a Semitic race just like the Arabs. How else would there be a word like anti-Semitic? I personally don't follow any organized religion, but both my parents were raised in Orthodox homes.

My beloved nanny was born in Ireland, but no one ever called her "Irish American." I think the only time she needed to write down that information was when she applied for citizenship. Of course, her brogue always gave her away, just as my grandson-in-law's British accent identifies him. My brother-in-law insists that he has no French accent left, but I always know it's he on the phone from the time he says hello. In his case, though, I find it interesting that it's not the pronunciation that exposes him, but the rhythm of his speech.

The same goes for my daughter, who moved to California about fifteen years ago, but still speaks with a New York rhythm. My son, on the other hand, has no regional accent of any kind, but he has a great ear and will often call me up pretending to be any one of the males I know. And he fools me every time! Oh, by the way, even though he was born here in New York, I guess I'm supposed to call him an Italian Jewish American.

Sex and The Silly

I'm not sure what was so shocking in the silent movies to warrant censorship — certainly nothing I've seen in the ones I've viewed, but when it did come in with much fanfare and diligence, it was absolutely ridiculous. I didn't know *any* married couples who slept in twin beds separated by a night table, and to this day I don't know anyone who carefully stops to put on a bathrobe before investigating a loud noise or crash in the house.

Personally, I have no interest in porn, but I see no reason why anyone who does shouldn't watch it if they so desire. I *do* have strong objections to anything that promotes pedophilia or excessive violence. The former should be firmly outlawed, and the second one needs regulating.

As far as nudity goes, for a time there was an argument about what was titillation and what was art. I think it finally boiled down to something inanimate was art, and someone who moved was obscene.

I still question shows or movies that toss in nudity for no real reason, and I also suspect actors who say they'll do "anything for their art."

Take the beautifully produced series *Homicide, Life on the Street* back in 1993. Although we'd get a quick long shot of the body to ascertain what had been found, we never saw a close-up detail. What we saw instead was the look of horror, pain, disgust and anger on the faces of the very talented actors. We certainly felt what they were portraying, but we didn't have to see it for ourselves.

Although I'm a passionate fan of Chris Meloni and thought his depiction of pure evil in the *Oz* series from 1997 was absolutely masterful, I felt that the frontal nudity shot of him at the end, where he's either mocking or trying to seduce the guard, was completely unnecessary. The focus of her eyes and the expression on her face told us what she was looking at. As much as I admire Mr. Meloni, I really didn't need to know him *that* well.

The same goes for a play I saw where an actor emerged from a bathtub for no reason whatsoever and got out facing the audience. The scene could have opened without his bath at all. What it did was set the audience to buzzing instead of immediately listening to the dialogue that followed.

To me graphic sex scenes in movies that are not listed as "porn" are most definitely inserted to entice audiences. I find it distracting, because while watching those scenes, I'm not thinking about the characters, but musing about the actors and wondering if and how much they were attracted to each other and what it led to.

Sometimes nudity on the stage is not at all contrived, but natural for the environment of the play. I think this is true of *Love, Valour and Compassion*. Upon leaving the theatre I found myself still concerned about the characters, not the actors.

Of course, the ultimate inducement for an audience was the utterly nude *Oh! Calcutta*. It was a dreadful revue with extremely unfunny sketches and some of the actors were equally unattractive. But the theatre would be filled. Why? Hasn't anyone ever looked at him/herself and his/her lover? Do they expect anything human to be *so* different as to arouse their… curiosity?

To Soothe The Savage Breast

After my partnership with my former lyricist was dissolved, and I had begun writing my own lyrics, I was looking around for a project and answered a request in The Dramatists Guild newsletter, which read, "Seeking a composer to collaborate on a musical version of a well-known film. Some of the lyrics are already written, but not in stone."

I called immediately and was asked to send a sample of my work, in exchange for which I naturally expected an example of a scene or two from the book writer.

"This is my first play," she announced. "I have been working in the academic area."

RED FLAG, Janet! STOP HERE! But I didn't.

"Well, what is the project?"

"Oh, I can't tell you that. I need to know that your music would be suitable, so that we could sign a partnership agreement, and I would be sure my idea was safe!"

"Oh, I see. The problem is I would write entirely different music for a period or historical piece than I would for something current. Can you give me a hint?"

"I guess you might as well know, but do you promise not to appropriate it for yourself alone?"

"Oh, you have my word," I assured her.

She then sent me an outline for what she would write based on a very popular movie that had had several sequels, and she included two of her lyrics.

I tidied up her rather sloppy renditions and set them to music, explaining that I would really prefer to write both the words and music myself.

She was apparently thrilled with the result, but commented that she "could rhyme all day," *kiss of death* for a would-be lyricist who thinks there's nothing to a lyric except a rhyme.

"Okay," she said. "Let's get started."
"By the way," I asked. "How did you get the rights from the studio?"
"Oh, I don't have the rights yet; I'm going to send them our tape."
I stopped answering ads.

Socializing

Where is the commandment that friends *must* find a new companion for someone who is recently divorced? People who are widowed are at least given a time for grieving, but the newly divorced are fair game.

My sisters and I had a family word, *jenk*, which described a person who was partly a jerk and partly a square. This had nothing to do with whether or not they were in show business. There are plenty of jenks in show business as in any other business.

In our family, however, we were often faced with a jenk who, upon being introduced, would clap his hands and sing the title of "If You Knew Susie." This was not only *not* endearing, but a tipoff of where the conversation was going from there.

I could never be as polite as my sister Natalie, but was inclined to answer the question "Mind if I smoke?" with the old chestnut, "Don't care if you burn" and discourage the jenks as quickly as possible. One of my "friends," in fixing me up, went on and on about how beautiful and talented the widower's wife had been and what a hard act she was to follow. He, it turned out, was not only downright ugly, but a jenk of the first order, and when he took me home, I had my key ready and bolted from the car, calling out a "thank you" and going inside as fast as I could.

Natalie was always shy and very soft spoken in public, but at home she was sardonic, playful and funny. She was tired of blind dates and usually refused to be "fixed up," but one of her friends made an offer she couldn't refuse. Her "date" had a single friend and wondered if Natalie also knew someone who would make up a foursome.

Natalie called her best friend, Jeannie, who agreed that this might turn out to be a pleasant evening. The gentlemen picked them up at their respective houses, and they met at a lovely restaurant at the appointed time. The men were average looking, but well dressed and had impeccable manners.

The first few minutes were awkward, as usual, and since both Natalie and Jeannie were both light drinkers, they each had one glass of wine, advising their dates not to order a full bottle. The dinner was excellent, but the conversation would start weakly and then drop like a cinder block. The women tried music, books, movies and even politics, but both men answered in bland, dull remarks or outright clichés.

The restaurant had a small dance floor and a band, and the four of them left the table to participate. To the women's horror, both men began singing along softly in their ears. Where this might have been romantic if they had been lovers and had a special song, it was, instead, the height of jenkiness, and Natalie and Jeannie had had it.

Fortunately, as the two couples edged closer to each other, one of the men suggested, "Let's change partners." Natalie winked at Jeannie, and Jeannie understood.

As the men released them, the women clasped each other and glided quickly off the floor and into the ladies room!

Underground Adventures

Many years ago my son-in-law was working as a bodyguard to various celebrities and therefore carried a licensed gun. He was returning home on the subway very late one night when he found himself alone in the car with four teenagers who were obviously up to no good. He had been trained to spot possible attackers and quickly thought of a solution. Without ever confronting them, he strolled over to the window at the end of the car and calmly looked straight out, as he casually stuck his hand in his pocket and managed to raise up his jacket so that his gun and holster were visible. The kids, who had been slowly moving towards him, got off at the next stop.

My late husband, already advanced in years, was sitting in a crowded subway car fairly early in the evening when a maniac came over and put an open scissors to his throat, instructing the passengers to put their money and jewelry into the bag he had left open next to him or he would slit my husband's throat. As they all nervously complied, one of the passengers was able to use his cell phone, and the crazed robber was apprehended at the next stop.

When he was just starting out, my son had been performing his songs at Pip's in Sheepshead Bay, and he used to dread the long subway ride home very late at night. On one of those nights he found himself alone in the car except for one other young man — also long haired and casually dressed, but seeming to be staring at him directly for several minutes. Finally, he strode over to where my son was sitting, and Brian thought, "Oh, God, he probably has a knife and there goes my pay and my guitar."

"You a musician?" the stranger asked.

"Uh-huh."

"So am I. I just got off work and I hate havin' to go back home at this hour."

They shook hands and gabbed the rest of the way into Manhattan.

I was on a crowded subway going to 34th Street to get a train to New Jersey, and I was hanging on to the pole not because there were no seats, but because I was getting off at the next stop. Some nice (and I hate to say it about my fellow New Yorkers) old-fashioned gentleman got up to give me his seat. I wanted to acknowledge his gesture by taking the seat, but the subway jerked to a halt, and I fell backwards. Three seated passengers put out their arms and not only caught me, but in the same movement put me back on my feet. I graciously thanked everyone and did indeed get off at my stop. Michael Bennett couldn't have choreographed it better.

Independence Day

"I was on my way to have an abortion when I thought 'What the hell? Maybe it'll be a girl this time.'"

That was the first full sentence I ever heard from my neighbor. We had both lived in the same building for some time, but had just spoken the usual polite greetings in the elevator from time to time. We were sitting side by side on a bench in a playground, watching our children in the sandbox. My son, Brian, was not quite two.

"That's my daughter, Patty, she's three. I have a son, Arty, in high school and another son, Harvey, in the first grade. I have to get home soon to make dinner for Nat, my husband, and the kids. No one likes the same things, so I make three different meals every night."

I nodded sympathetically, but didn't know what to say. She wasn't waiting for an answer, however. She was worried about how to get Patty out of the park, because she kicked and screamed and threw sand at her mother.

From that day on she would capture me for apologies wherever we happened to meet. In the market it was "So what could I do — I bought a chicken." In the drugstore it was "I couldn't help it — I had to get some aspirin for Nat." In the local kids' clothing store it was "Harvey is growing so fast I just had to get him new pants."

She was basically a pretty woman with naturally blonde hair and a tidy figure, but she apparently never had time for makeup or for shopping for herself and wore only plain housedresses and sturdy shoes.

One night my husband and I were relaxing and catching up on the news. Little Brian had been asleep for a couple of hours. Suddenly, our doorbell rang, and my husband cautiously looked through the peephole. It was our neighbor, Mary, asking if she could come in.

"Of course," he said. "Is anything wrong?"

"Oh, no," she answered quickly. "I just hoped you were home. Nat is playing poker at his friend's house; Arty has a date; Patty is asleep, and Harvey is stuck in the bathroom."

"Did you want help to get him out?" I asked.

"Oh, no! He was taking a bath, and when he got out of the tub, he wanted to open the door to let the steam out, but the knob is glass, and I guess he pulled on it too hard, so it came out and crashed to the floor in little pieces. When he called out to me, I told him to pick up each little piece, because he's barefoot and could cut his feet. I figure that'll take about an hour, so I came down for a little visit."

She chattered on and on and was funny and surprisingly interesting. Her family were not ogres; they just took her for granted, just as she took her role of slave for granted, and no one ever considered a change.

Flash forward to Nat's passing, Arty's marriage and Harvey's and Patty's scholarships to good colleges from their remarkably high grades.

Mary didn't know what to do with her freedom, so she had a serious heart attack. Her kids all lovingly pulled her through and offered her a place in any one of their homes. She chose to live in her own apartment — a smaller one than she had lived in for all the time I knew her — and did so for many years thereafter.

I could never have predicted that reverse ending even if I had a crystal ball.

Insurance

Many years ago I was conversing with a very nice man at a party, and we began to swap kid stories. I told him about the horrible experience I had when my daughter was about four years old.

I had taken her Christmas shopping with me and didn't realize we'd be heading home on the subway at rush hour. Because I was carrying so many packages, I told her to hang on to my coat pocket instead of my hand, but as we made our way through the crowd, she lost her grip, and we were separated by swarms of people determined to catch their trains.

As I looked down and didn't see her hanging on to me, I felt absolute panic and began to search wildly, hoping no train would come along. We were on the platform that accommodated the express on one side and the local on the other, which made it even more difficult to concentrate.

Finally, as both trains came along and the crowd thinned out, I spotted her at the end of the platform, standing absolutely still with the tears pouring down her face.

Fortunately, she had really listened to my warning, which I had repeated every time we went anywhere: *If we should ever get separated, don't get on any train, don't go off with any stranger (even one in a uniform) and don't look for me; I will find you.*

The other party guest nodded sympathetically, but said, with a grin, that it was a shame I hadn't had his insurance. It seemed that he and his wife had taken their twin daughters to an amusement park when their children, too, were about four years of age. While waiting to get on a ride, one of them wandered off unnoticed, and after a quick desperate search, he and his wife, together with the remaining twin, went to the Lost Children booth. It was very well equipped, containing a loud speaker and a closed-circuit, very large television monitor. The man in charge asked for a description of the child and said they could zoom in on a wallet picture, if necessary.

"She looks like *this*," the father said, holding up the other twin. Within not more than five minutes, a young woman walked into the booth with her own child in one hand and the missing twin in the other.

"Our kids have been playing together for the past twenty minutes," she said. "I didn't know she was lost; I thought her parents were probably nearby. When I heard the announcement and saw her image, I came as fast as I could."

I guess it's always good to carry a spare.

Take A Letter

In my senior year in high school I switched from a college prep course to a business course, longing for my independence more than further education. One day a notice was circulated throughout the commercial class that a local real estate office was looking for a part-time switchboard operator/stenographer. The pay was $10 a week *and* it would count as a full academic credit.

Not a single hand was raised except mine, so an interview was arranged with George E. Reade of Reade & Wright Real Estate. Mr. Wright was deceased, but the catchy name remained.

At the end of my morning classes, which now eliminated study hall and gym and substituted my most important afternoon classes, I was to meet Mr. Reade, and I was hired on the spot. Every day I would bring a sandwich, because when I relieved the regular switchboard operator/receptionist, there would be very few calls during the lunch hour. In fact, most of Beverly Hills had the same lunch hour!

The office was a loft with glass cubicles for each of the brokers and a large glass-enclosed office in the back for Mr. Reade. He was the image of Abe Vigoda, a kindly man with a bombastic temper when it came to business, and most of the time, when he would call "Janet," I'd walk back with my steno pad for dictation, but sometimes he'd be on the phone (private, not connected to the switchboard), and if he disagreed with a proposed deal, he might yell "Damn it!" so loudly that I'd think he said "Janet" and come running with my shorthand book.

When he and all the other brokers were out, my sister Natalie would often call to chat with me, and we used the same dopey joke every time. "Good afternoon, this is Reade and Wright." "Good afternoon, this is Arithmetic!" Because I was the chattier one, Natalie confessed to me years later that as I rattled on and on, she would put down the phone and clean her entire house, picking up the instrument every now and then with an "Uh-huh."

I refused an allowance, since I was now a wage earner, and although it made my father laugh, I think he was proud of me.

By the time I graduated, I had saved enough for a ticket to go back home to New York to live, and one of my friends decided to try her luck also. We shared a tiny studio apartment and both got secretarial jobs in the same company, close enough so that we could walk to work and home and save bus fare.

It was a very happy time for me except for the early morning hours. I'll always be a night owl, so I could never go to sleep when I should have, and that alarm clock was like an army bugle call to me. I made up for it by clocking in, making sure my boss hadn't yet arrived and going down to the snack bar for a jelly doughnut and two cups of coffee!

In school I had been rather shy, and although I had many friends and spoke up when called upon in class, I never purposely drew attention to myself, but I was giddy with my freedom of living on my own and not being known only as someone's daughter. I'm afraid I did become the office clown.

Board meetings were held only in the morning or after lunch, so because the board room was not in use when we secretaries would open our "brown bags," we'd congregate around the long table to eat and exchange stories or jokes — or sometimes gripes.

I was finding that I was getting more and more laughs at my tall tales and mimicry, and my reticence became a thing of the past. My colleagues were egging me on, and lunch time became show time!

One day I did a particularly long routine, but after everyone else had stopped laughing, one of the young girls went on howling hysterically, with tears streaming down her face.

"Wow," I thought. "Maybe I should do this professionally."

It was then that everyone felt that they should call the company doctor, and it was discovered that she had just recently been released from a mental hospital; this was her first job.

I never again tried to "lay 'em in the aisles."

There's No Business Like…

My husband was cursed with a major problem: too much talent!

As a child he appeared in vaudeville and fell in love with the theatre. That was the one area where he was happiest. However, he was encouraged to go to art school, so that he could always make a living doing commercial art, which he never really enjoyed.

Instead, he auditioned cold for various Broadway shows and got every job he went for, because he had taught himself to dance and could pick up on any choreography with which he was confronted. He even learned Hindu dancing, which is particularly difficult because it requires the simultaneous use of your hands, your fingers, your head and all the rest of your body in precise movements. As a Hindu dancer, he worked with the then-famous Beatrice Kraft.

After his stint with her was over, he went on to appear on television and in cabaret, but when he was "at liberty," he not only paid his rent with commercial art, but began serious painting, turning his single rented room into a studio.

Thus it went, back and forth between art and the theatre. He had several successful one-man shows and even painted the portrait of Judy Garland that hung in the Palace Theatre and was finally acquired by the Museum of the City of New York.

Sadly, he never stayed with either profession long enough to make it to the top, and after we were married and starting a family, he decided to go the business route. One of our closest friends was in the garment business, and when Gari, as he called himself, showed him some dresses he had designed, they came up with the idea of going into business for themselves — with Seymour, our friend, handling the operation and Gari creating the designs.

Seymour found a willing third partner to make the patterns and have the samples sewn. He had a very small factory in Queens and said he could handle small orders successfully as the business grew. He also had the space to store the fabrics.

All the samples were made in my size, as I was their only model. At first things seemed to be going well, but it was foolish to think they could really make a go of it on a shoestring. When our son, Brian, was a baby, I had to park him somewhere if we were going to see the buyers at Bloomingdale's or Macy's (both of which gave us orders). My aunt lived just ten blocks from where we did, and one morning we asked her to wait on her corner as we came by in a cab. We told the cab to wait, as we opened the door and handed her the baby, and then we took off. It was a strange feeling — as if we had just sold him!

Besides the orders from the department stores and a couple of boutiques, Loretta Young wore one of the designs on her television show, with a "Gari" credit.

With those orders coming in, our hopes were high, but the factory was slow in responding, and one day we decided to go out to Queens and see what was holding things up.

It was Gari and Seymour who were held up. The factory was vacant, and all the patterns and fabrics had disappeared, never to be found again.

So much for playing it safe.

Ladies Who Lunch

Lucille and I have been friends for about sixty years! We met in the playground while watching our kids. When both of our husbands were alive, we spent many a delightful evening together, since her husband, a composer, could play any song by ear and my husband loved to sing.

When her son, Jonathan, grew up, he became my jazz teacher, and today, besides all his other activities, I still think he's the best music teacher in New York.

Lucille was singing in the City Opera chorus, and I was learning to write both words and music for theatre, although I did write only the lyrics for songs I wrote with Marvin, her husband.

Now she's a grandmother, and I'm a great-grandmother, and we have more time for lunch, although we often went to concerts, theatre and lectures together over the years.

Shortly before the following perilous experience, she had a pacemaker inserted, and I had a triple bypass. We were both feeling fine and looked forward to going way downtown to the book signing by my brother-in-law, Robert Clary.

We had carefully planned to travel early because of the weather warning of a storm, and we ate lunch in a lovely little restaurant in the park — just a short walk from where the event was being held. We had just finished when the sky began turning darker and darker, and we asked directions to the building. To our great distress, we were mistakenly told to go the "long" way, which meant actually circling the park instead of going straight ahead on a very short path.

Almost immediately the clouds burst, and we didn't know where to turn for shelter. The powerful wind and the relentless rain made it almost impossible to move. On one side of the path was a railing, and we felt maybe we could hang on and go forward. We grabbed each other's hands and tried to cross. Lucille made it, but my hand slipped out of hers, and there I was — up against a tree and helpless.

Suddenly, a man appeared from nowhere, understood my plight and took hold of my shoulders, practically carrying me across the path. I thanked him profusely and held onto the railing with all my might. Lucille was right in front of me, and we edged our way all around the park to the back entrance of the premises. There we found a deep puddle right in front of the two steps to the door. With no other alternative, we stepped into the puddle and finally reached the steps.

As we walked through the door, dripping wet from head to toe and almost completely out of breath, we saw Robert in the lobby, milling around with those who had also avoided the storm. When he caught sight of us, he came over and looked a bit shocked. Since the curtains had been drawn and the bright lights were blazing, he had no idea of what was going on outside.

"Well, hello, you two. You certainly cut it close. I go on in about a minute, but that should give you time to comb your hair and put on some lipstick. You look *awful!*"

Scrabble

Where is our language going? We acquired it from the English and made it our own by mixing in various words and phrases from the immigrants who incorporated their own cultures when they came here for refuge.

Kids have always used crutches. In my day it was "super," and today it's "awesome," but what saddens and mystifies me is that the adults are also depending upon the overused phrase.

In school we were required to learn a new word every day. Of course, we didn't remember them all or use them as frequently as our teachers would have liked, but we also had reading requirements, which some of us enjoyed immensely and did indeed expand our vocabularies.

I came from a household of readers, and the advent of television didn't affect our love of books. There's still something magical in imagining what a character looks like or is feeling without having it done for us.

There was a time when it was taken for granted that newscasters were the ones to pronounce and define words correctly, not to mention using impeccable grammar, but today they, too, have allowed serious changes to take place. The worst offense, to me, is saying that something is different "than." "Different" is not a comparative. There's no such thing as "different, differenter, differentest!" Things can be only different "from."

Rap is nothing new. It was simply called "patter" when it was first used in the theatre. The enormous contrast is that when professional lyricists wrote patter, they used true rhymes and made sense; it wasn't based on outcries of an angry person spouting off. The blues took care of that beautifully. What's more, it was not called music, because there was, and still isn't, anything melodic involved. It is a collection of spoken words to a beat.

In mentioning "true rhymes," I refer to things like "mine" and "wine," not "mine" and "time." In discussing it with other lyricists, I have often heard the argument that "there was no other way to get across the meaning." *Yes, there is!* Rearrange your words so that you're still saying the same thing, but the word that is to be rhymed is a different one. This is *always* possible; it just takes a little more effort.

Getting back to our daily use of language, I think the Internet should bear some of the blame. The shortcut speech patterns don't require any contemplation, and individuality is becoming a thing of the past.

There was one word coined in the fifties of which I am extremely fond and will always use when the need arises. The jazz musicians' "dig" is a favorite of mine, because I actually can't think of another word that combines comprehend, empathize and prefer.

Also of jazz origin is "cool," but that comes and goes and doesn't seem to be a staple.

I don't know how definitions change, however. In my day "busted" meant broke, as in down and out. How it got to mean "arrested" no one has explained.

And speaking of "busted," in the days when it was unthinkable to use the word "breast," it was perfectly fine to refer to a woman's breasts as her "bust." Neither female nor male genitals were ever referred to in polite society except, when absolutely necessary, as "down there!"

With all the pejorative words referring to homosexuals banished, I will never understand why "gay" is okay. Are they to be considered a merry band? A carefree community? Or is it sarcastic and rather cynical? Since gays use the word themselves, they must feel comfortable with it, but I think I would have preferred something more dignified. To each his own, I guess.

To sum it up, we have so many delicious words at our disposal that I think it's a real shame that we limit ourselves to the current clichés.

Why, it's positively awesome!

Jumping The Gun

When I was first married, I was working as the secretary to the head of a theatrical union. He was a glad-to-meetcha guy, very personable, but totally incapable of any fundamental service that needed to be done for the union.

Work was a five-and-a-half-day schedule in those days, so I was also expected to come in on Saturday mornings. One Saturday he announced that he would be dictating his annual report to the membership and that we would be busy through lunch, so he would send out. His assistant, a young, very nice fellow, who *did* have a brain, would join us later.

We wrote and rewrote all morning, but when our sandwiches arrived, he decided to go out to lunch after all. I ate my sandwich and finished typing up everything we had written so far (correcting his very bad grammar, which he never noticed).

He returned with a strange look on his face and called me into his office without my steno pad.

Before continuing, I should explain what preceded this. If you've ever heard someone say, "Stop yelling; you'll burst a blood vessel," you probably thought, as I did, that it was simply an exaggeration. Well, it isn't! My father had been rehearsing and had had to hit a very high note over and over again, and he had indeed burst a blood vessel. The doctor informed him that it would heal in a very short time, but only if he did not use his vocal chords at all — not to speak or even whisper, and he admitted him to a hospital, equipped with a pad and pencil, to be sure he followed orders.

My boss told me to sit down and began to hem and haw. "What is it?" I asked, already somewhat shaken.

"I know your mother and one of your sisters are in town; can you reach them?"

"Why? Is something wrong with my father?"

He nodded, adding in a low, respectful tone, "He's gone."

"You mean he's *dead*?" I shouted.

"I'm afraid so."

I burst into tears just as his assistant walked in the door. "What's going on?" he asked.

"I just told her the news about her father."

"What news?"

"That he has passed."

"How do you know?"

"Well, the word is all over the street."

"You mean you didn't even *check*?"

Without waiting for an answer, he asked me if I had the phone number of the hospital room and told me to call there immediately.

I did, and I heard lots of tapping on the other end of the phone.

"Daddy, *is that you?*" I cried.

There was a lot more frantic tapping, and I told him I'd be right over.

I rushed out, leaving my overeager boss to deal with his level-headed assistant.

When I entered my father's hospital room, I found him looking rested and very healthy, as he sat at a desk, writing. Although I was now an adult and too big to fit, I jumped into his lap and kissed his cheeks over and over, getting his face all wet with my tears.

"What's the matter?" he scribbled on the pad.

When I told him, he wrote the Yiddish word for "one who relishes bringing bad news."

I went back to the office on Monday and finished up the report in time for the presentation. My boss apologized, but I had trouble being even civil to him after that. Actually, I stayed at that job until two weeks before my son, Brian, was born, and I couldn't fit behind my desk any longer. Gee, if he had been born in that office, he would have been on Broadway thirty-five years before he got there with his show, "Late Nite Comic!"

Where's My Parachute?

Every summer when my kids were little, we would travel from our home in New York to visit my family in California. My husband never did catch on to the time difference, so he would insist that we get an early morning flight, which meant arriving in California practically before we left!

It was always a nerve-wracking procedure to get the kids ready, turn off every appliance that needed to be unplugged and to get a cab to the airport.

One morning everything seemed to be fighting us. The cab driver managed to get lost in the Bronx, and it took him ages to find his way out. Then he got a flat tire and had to flag down another cab for us to proceed.

When we finally reached the airport, we literally ran to the waiting area for our flight, but there was a notice that it had been delayed. We sat there catching our breath and sat and sat and sat. All the passengers were getting edgy, especially those traveling on business, and one by one they would approach the desk for information.

The answer was always the same: "There will be an announcement as soon as we get further word."

Of course, everyone was picturing the same thing — a plane so badly in need of repair that they just couldn't seem to fix it. Would it really be safe to board?

After waiting for about an hour and a half, my husband strolled over to the desk and began to chat with the agent. When he felt they were palsy-walsy enough, he leaned over the counter and asked — very confidentially, "What is *really* going on?"

The man behind the counter actually blushed.

"Someone forgot to schedule a plane; we're waiting for one to come in from Chicago and reload!"

The Way To Whose Heart?

"My mother is a terrible cook." That was the opening line to the preface in one of my sister Edna's published cookbooks.

And true it was. When my first two sisters were born and my father was on the road, Mother lived with her married sister who did all the cooking. By the time Edna came along, my father was doing well enough for them to get their own little house and hire a cook.

Therefore none of us learned to cook "by my mother's knee" — we didn't learn to cook at all! We all learned to bake, because we were addicted to sweets. Margie's pot de crème was sensational, and Natalie's tarte de pomme was delicious and looked exactly like the photograph in the French cookbook she utilized. I still use Edna's brownie recipe. Marilyn made terrible fudge that never congealed, but I loved it and ate it with a spoon.

Margie never married and therefore never had to make anything but great desserts when she'd go to our folks' or to any of her sisters'. Natalie had to learn from scratch when she got married, and she assumed following any other recipe would be as easy as making her sumptuous cakes. Not quite. The first roast she attempted required basting every half hour with a cup of hot water, but she didn't understand that the one cup of water listed in the ingredients meant just that — *one* cup throughout the cooking time. She therefore added a full cup of water every half hour until the roast was swimming in the pan instead of baking.

Edna was always experimenting with food, so learning to cook like the gourmet she became was not difficult.

Marilyn was fortunate, like me, to have a husband who knew how to cook, but when she got married, she took a cooking course, where she learned to make three elegant dishes and, I guess, kept rotating them!

I was eighteen when I met my future husband, and I had a roommate who knew only a smidgen more than I did about cooking. We thought it would be very romantic to invite him to dinner, so she prepared four hamburger patties for me to cook and diplomatically went out to dinner herself. I knew he liked onion in his hamburgers, so off I went to the market. The problem was that I had never shopped for food, and I mistook an entire bulb of garlic for an onion. I chopped it up carefully and combined it into the four patties. He happened to have a bad cold, but I think I opened his sinuses forever!

No one would come near us for weeks, but that didn't stop me. My next attempt was breaded veal cutlets, which I knew was one of his favorites. He arrived early to ask if he could do anything to help and found me tearing up a piece of white bread and trying desperately to make it stick to a cutlet. When he could stop laughing, he said he'd be right back and returned with a container of bread crumbs and a dozen eggs. He showed me how to dip the cutlet into egg and then bread crumbs, and he basically made the dinner himself.

For the first year we were married, he was either at home painting or out doing commercial art in various locations. I was working in an office, but he always got home earlier than I did. We lived on the second floor of a brownstone, and what a delight it was to climb the stairs and smell something tantalizing for dinner. Of course, once we had a baby, and I had learned to cook, he abdicated as chief chef, but when we would visit in California for the summer, and my sister Margie would drop in now and then in the evening, he would come up with a great snack using whatever was in the refrigerator. She dubbed him "the best short order cook in the country."

Efficiency

When I first met my future husband, he introduced me to many of his friends, including a very beautiful young woman from whom I later rented an apartment. She was not a particular favorite of mine, nor of any of his other friends, but she was very smart and lovely to look at, and somehow he was able to ignore her distasteful nature. She was conniving and greedy and true to no one, but she could turn on the charm when she wanted to.

When she commissioned him to paint her portrait, he did his usual spectacular job, but because of his insightful renditions, he didn't even realize that the hands she had placed in her lap came out looking more like claws. Neither of them noticed, and she hung the painting in a prominent place in her apartment.

At the time, besides renting out real estate that she owned, she was working for an anti-Semitic organization. She had no ill feeling whatsoever against Jews, but the job paid very well, and that was her prime objective at all times.

Meanwhile, my young friend who used to disappear over the summer decided to stay in town. He heard that her organization was gaining traction with its outrageous mailings and immediately applied for a job as a file clerk.

He was not Jewish himself — just a decent human being, and he would arrive every morning, bright and chipper, and check out at the end of the day, receiving his weekly paycheck nonchalantly.

By the end of the summer, however, he had deliberately screwed up the files so badly that — for quite a while, at least, the organization was at a standstill.

Where Celldom Is Heard

I carry a cell phone only for emergencies, preferring to chat at home on my land line. Before I had one, however, I thought everyone had gone crazy and were talking to themselves on the street. Some people can't do without one — just as they can't leave their homes without a bottle of water. No wonder everyone now carries a large shoulder bag or wears a backpack.

I must admit I understand what a time saver it is for my family. My daughter calls me from her gym when she's on the treadmill. Since that leaves her always a little breathless, I don't know how I'll ever distinguish if she's calling with world-shaking news.

My granddaughter calls from the car, because the motion makes her two little babies fall asleep, and that's the only time she has to talk. Her husband calls me from his car when he leaves work, and we have long conversations until he gets home and pulls into the driveway.

Most of the time I suspect my son doesn't really need to call me from the street, but he can't bear wasting time as he's walking home from a restaurant or a business appointment. I always get a laugh out of his nearly jumping out of his skin if he gets a call in a restaurant. He keeps the phone on "vibrate," and when he's not expecting a call, he thinks he's being electrocuted.

He has found a particularly inventive use, however. Being a songwriter and usually writing both the words and music simultaneously, he doesn't want to lose a thought when he's not at home at the piano, so he takes out his cell phone, punches in his home phone and sings into it while the inspiration is compelling. When he arrives home, there is the new song on his phone machine, waiting for completion.

A cell has come in very handy if I've been wearing headphones and haven't heard my doorbell ring. My friends know to call me, because one of my phones not only has a loud ring, but also lights up, and I can then go let them in.

The funniest situation I was ever in was when I was on a bus going through a traverse tunnel in Central Park. Apparently, a truck had entered at Fifth Avenue, ignoring the sign stating the lawful height of a vehicle. It had somehow gotten through to about the middle when it got stuck, its roof scraping the inside of the tunnel, but keeping it from going any further. Our bus had also entered, because the truck couldn't be seen at the entrance, and we were followed by one or two cars.

There was no way for all of us to back out, so the bus driver called for help, which meant waiting until some kind of machine and workmen arrived who could literally shear off the top of the truck and release it. It was obvious that this was going to take at least an hour, if not more, and it was dinner time.

Suddenly, cell phones popped out of everywhere — all with the same message.

"I'm going to be a little late, dear."

The Twilight Zone

The brownstone in which we lived when I was first married had obviously been the residence of one family, but had been broken up into two peculiarly-shaped apartments per floor. I assume our second-floor apartment had been the parlor.

It consisted of a large living room with a bay window and a hastily constructed tiny kitchen adjacent to a tiny bathroom. The bedroom had not existed at all and was separated from the living room by a double glass-paned door. I had not bothered to make curtains for the door, because no one would be there when we were sleeping, and if we had guests, the doors were left open so that coats could be piled on our bed.

In the six months we had been living there, no one had put up the required window shade in the bedroom, so the moonlight filled the room and actually lit it up. We put an armoire next to the window as a closet and a bureau next to the bed as a nightstand. There was not an inch of space for anything else.

Every Saturday night someone's horn would get stuck, and it seemed like ages before a cop would dismantle it. It would wake us, of course, but I would usually fall right back to sleep. One hot summer night, however, when we were sleeping in as little as possible, I didn't see my husband get out of bed and head for the kitchen for a drink of water. As I looked through the glass doors to the dimly-lit living room, all I saw was a half-naked man walking through our living room, and in panic I was about to call the police, when my husband came back into the bedroom and asked what was wrong. I told him, and he quickly donned a robe and went searching for the intruder, but when he checked the locks and found nothing had been disturbed, he figured out that it was he I had seen, and he came back to bed to reassure me.

By coincidence, the next morning the elderly super with his even older large dog entered quietly with the house key and walked directly into our bedroom. I don't know where he was from, so I couldn't identify the accent, but he said calmly, "I take the mazzures" and proceeded to put up a ladder. When he had ascertained the dimensions of the shade, he turned to us and said, "You have a good Zunday" and left.

We were sure we had no more surprises, but one day when I was putting the garbage on the dumb waiter, which we would deliver to the basement on a pulley, and which the super would empty and send the pail back up to us, I opened the door and found myself facing the housewife from the adjoining apartment. We were both taken aback by this unexpected meeting, but we had a lovely chat, and the four of us became good friends, giving birth to our first babies just one week apart. We remained friends until they moved to the suburbs, and getting together was no longer easily accessible.

In our ninth month of pregnancy we had even shared a Peeping Tom from across the street who used to watch us with binoculars whenever our husbands would take a night off and go to the movies. We laughed and waved at him good naturedly, feeling sorry for him that he couldn't find more shapely neighbors on which to spy.

The Hills Are Alive...

What fun it was to watch the 1937 movie *The Hurricane* recently. My best friend, Adina, and I were ten when we first saw it, and we took turns playing the parts of Dorothy Lamour and Jon Hall. As Lamour, we would tie ourselves to the big tree in my backyard, shouting, "Get to the church! Get to the church!"

Then, as Jon Hall, we would jump into the pool and swim the length underwater as we made our "escape."

As I grew up and beyond the tree-climbing stage, I didn't give much thought to greenery of any kind, and I always felt that Joyce Kilmer's homage to a tree was highly overwrought.

Going beyond only playing the piano, I was beginning to study music itself; i.e., theory, harmony, composition and arranging. I found it too difficult to hold down a full-time job, so I looked for part-time work and found it right next door, where the brother of my music teacher owned a small advertising agency, and he needed someone to keep the books, design the brochures and send out the mailings, setting my own hours.

His wife had been a longtime friend of my husband's, so the four of us would frequently dine together. One night they revealed excitedly that they had built a house in Upstate New York and invited us to drive up with them for a weekend of country living with an indescribable view, assuring city girl me that the plumbing and heating had already been installed.

On a rainy day in October we put our overnight bags and my husband's painting equipment in the trunk of their car, and off we went.

It was a very long drive, and I was grateful when the car finally came to a stop with a cheerful "We're here!" from our hosts. I didn't see the house at first, because we were at the bottom of a steep hill, and the house was at the very top. We were lucky to have brought along boots, because we had to slog through deep mud while carrying our suitcases and bags of groceries for the weekend.

The house had been built as a copy of a medieval castle, and another brother of our host, who was in the antique business, had provided authentic furniture. It was very impressive, but after the long journey we were more interested in the lavatory facilities than anything else.

Well, two beautifully decorated bathrooms had indeed been built, but the plumbing had *not* yet been installed. We were placidly informed that we were to use the original outhouse that was still there on the hill.

Our next surprise was that the lovely kitchen had not yet been connected to a water line, which made it necessary to pump water from the well outside and bring it in for any cooking purposes. Of course, this meant that there was also no gas or electricity. Our hostess had made a stew at home in the city and heated it in a kettle hanging over the fireplace in the large front room. This huge fireplace heated the entire front part of the house, including the loft where my husband and I were to sleep. The other bedroom, on the ground floor, had its own small fireplace.

The hot food and good red wine made us very sleepy after our unexpectedly active day, and we foolishly asked about how we were to brush our teeth while heading off to bed. "We never bother to bring our toothbrushes," our hosts chuckled. We figured it was probably a good idea to make our way to the outhouse and back before climbing the ladder to the loft.

There were twin beds, both made up with two blankets each, but the fire in the big room was beginning to die down, and the cold was becoming more intense. We quickly gave up the idea of putting on our nightclothes, piled all the blankets on one bed, plus our coats, and huddled together, hoping for sleep.

When we finally did drift off, we were awakened by a cry from our hosts: "The aurora borealis! Quick! Look out the window!"

We looked. We saw. We crawled back to bed and under the covers.

The next day brought lots of sunshine and a perfect view of the "purple mountain majesties" below us.

My husband was inspired to bring his easel, canvas and paint halfway down the hill and begin sketching. At lunchtime I wrapped up a sandwich of thick homemade bread and delicious cheese and made my way down to where he was painting. I could hardly wait to take a peek.

There, instead of a rendering of the gorgeous trees and mountains, he was finishing an incredibly accurate portrait of a rainy street in New York, busy with taxi cabs, people and familiar buildings.

"I'm not one of the old masters," he explained. "I was so daunted by what I saw that I thought I'd better paint what I knew!"

Bear Manor Media

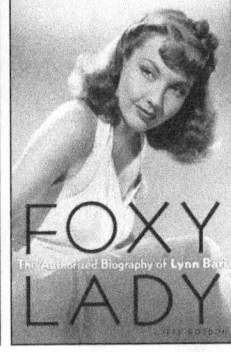

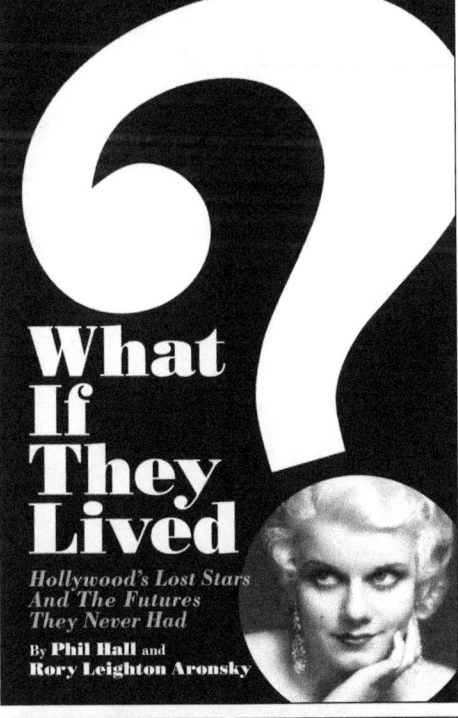

Classic Cinema.
Timeless TV.
Retro Radio.

WWW.BEARMANORMEDIA.COM

www.ingramcontent.com/pod-product-compliance
Lightning Source LLC
Chambersburg PA
CBHW051930160426
43198CB00012B/2091